P9-DMU-198

Elvis Is Dead And I Don't Feel So Good Myself

LEWIS GRIZZARD

PEACHTREE PUBLISHERS, LTD.

Published by
PEACHTREE PUBLISHERS, LTD.
494 Armour Circle, N.E.
Atlanta, Georgia 30324

Copyright © 1984 Lewis Grizzard

All rights reserved. No part of this book may be reproduced in any form
or by any means without the prior written permission of the Publisher,
excepting brief quotes used in connection with reviews, written specifically
for inclusion in a magazine or newspaper.

Manufactured in the United States of America

First printing

Library of Congress Catalog Number 84-60922

ISBN: 0-931948-66-5

Other books by Lewis Grizzard:

Kathy Sue Loudermilk, I Love You

Won't You Come Home, Billy Bob Bailey?

Don't Sit Under the Grits Tree With Anyone Else But Me

They Tore Out My Heart and Stomped That Sucker Flat

If Love Were Oil, I'd Be About A Quart Low

Dedication

To Danny Thompson, Bobby Entrekin, Mike Murphy, Dudley Stamps, Charles Moore, Clyde Elrod, Worm Elrod, and Anthony Yeager — the boys from Moreland, who I hope and pray didn't grow up to be as confused as I am.

And to the memory of Eddie Estes, a great centerfielder.

Elvis Is Dead And I Don't Feel So Good Myself

1 A Last Toast To The King

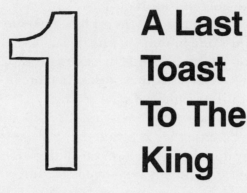

W E WERE SITTING on the beach in Hilton Head, South Carolina, me and Price and Franklin. We were mired in those squatty folding chairs, the kind the old people take down to the surf and sit in while the salt water splashes over them. We were drinking cold beer and acting our age.

You can always tell the approximate age of people by watching what they do when they go to the beach. Babies, of course, dabble in the sand and splash around in the shallow water.

When a kid is about ten or twelve, he goes out farther and rides the waves and balks at his mother's motions that it's time to leave.

"Come on, Timmy. It's time to go back to the motel."

"Can't we stay just a little bit longer?"

"No. Your daddy is ready to leave."

"But I want to swim some more."

"I said come here, young man."

"Let me ride just one more wave. Please?"

1

"Don't make me call your daddy."

"I'll ride just one more and then I'll be ready to go."

"Okay, but just one more."

Parents never win at the beach, at least in these permissive times they don't. A kid can always just-one-more his parents into another thirty minutes of wave riding.

When children become teen-agers, the girls stop going into the water because they're afraid they will get their hair wet. What they do instead is put on tiny little swimsuits and lie on towels getting tanned. Teen-aged boys throw frisbees.

There should be a law against throwing frisbees on beaches. In the first place, throwing a frisbee is a mindless exercise that can't be any fun whatsoever. After you've seen one frisbee float through the air, you've seen them all. They might as well try catching horseflies.

Also, on crowded beaches there isn't room for teen-aged boys to throw frisbees. Frisbees are difficult to control and difficult to catch, so they're always landing on people who are trying to relax in the sun. Sometimes, frisbees even knock over somebody's beer.

A kid knocked over my beer with a frisbee at the beach once. I threatened him with a lawsuit and then put this curse on him: "May your voice never change and your zits win prizes at county fairs." I hate it when somebody knocks over my beer at the beach.

When kids are college age, the girls still lie on towels getting tanned and worrying about getting their hair wet. The boys, meanwhile, have given up throwing frisbees and have joined the girls, lying next to them on their own towels.

They play loud rock music, and when the girls ask them to rub suntan oil on their backs, they enthusiastically oblige ... especially if the girl has unsnapped the back of her tiny top

2

and the boy knows that her breasts are unleashed, for all practical purposes. The beach habits of people this age are basically preliminary sexual exercises, but rarely do they lead to anything more advanced later in the day. As numerous studies have shown, it is quite uncomfortable to attempt to have sex after an afternoon of lying in the sun because of the unpleasant feeling that individuals get when they rub their sunburned skin against that of someone whose epidermis is in the same painful condition.

At about age thirty, most people have the good sense to stop frying their skin in the sun for hours. They know by then that having sex is more fun than having a sunburn; they have heeded all the reports about how lying in the sun causes skin cancer; and they are usually working on their first nervous breakdown by age thirty, and all they want to do at the beach is sit there and relax while drinking cold beer.

The three of us that day at Hilton Head had already tiptoed into our thirties and the beer was going down exceptionally well. I have no idea what women talk about when they're sitting on a beach together without any men around, but when no women are present, men talk about the physical attributes of everything that happens to walk past them — or is lying close to them on a towel — wearing a bikini.

Me and Price and Franklin were doing just that:

"Good God."

"Where?"

"Left."

"Good God."

"How old do you think she is?"

"Eighteen."

"No way. Sixteen."

"Did they look like that when we were sixteen?"

"They couldn't have."

"Why not?"

"If they had, I wouldn't have lived this long. Some daddy would have shot me."

"Yeah, and they got the pill today, too."

"I wonder if the boys their age know how lucky they are."

"They don't have any idea."

"Wonder how old they are when they start these days?"

"Rodney Dangerfield said the kids are doing it so young these days that his daughter bought a box of Cracker Jacks and the prize was a diaphragm."

"Great line."

"Look coming here."

"It's a land whale."

"Damn, she's fat."

"If somebody told her to haul ass, she'd have to make two trips."

"That's awful."

"Hey, we're out of beer."

I remember distinctly that it was Franklin who went back to the condo to get more beer. I also remember distinctly that the month was August and the year was 1977. We had the radio playing. It was a country station.

Franklin was gone thirty minutes. When he came back, he had another twelve-pack. He also had a troubled look on his face.

"What took you so long?" Price asked him. "You didn't call Sweet Thing back home, did you?"

"You're not going to believe what I just heard on television," he answered.

I had just taken the first pull on my fresh beer when I

4

heard him utter three incredible words.

"Elvis is dead," he said.

Elvis is dead. The words didn't fit somehow. The queen of England is dead. There has been a revolution in South America and the dictator is dead. Some rock singer has been found in his hotel room with a needle in his arm and he is dead. All that made sense, but not *Elvis is dead.*

"They figure he had a heart attack," said the bad news bearer.

A heart attack? Elvis Presley couldn't have a heart attack. He was too young to have a heart attack. He was too young to have anything like that. Elvis Presley was my idol when I was a kid. Elvis changed my life. Elvis turned on my entire generation. I saw *Love Me Tender* three times. He died in *Love Me Tender,* but that was just a movie.

I figured this was some sort of joke. Right, Elvis Presley had a heart attack. And where did they find his body? In Heartbreak Hotel, of course.

The music had stopped on the radio. A man was talking.

"Elvis Presley is dead," said the voice. "He was forty-two."

Forty-two? That had to be wrong, too. How could he be that old? Elvis had to be younger than that. He was one of us, wasn't he? If he was forty-two, maybe he could have had a heart attack. If he was over forty, that meant he probably had wrinkles and maybe his hair had already fallen out and he had been wearing a wig.

But if Elvis Presley was forty-two and old enough to die, what did that say about me and the generation he had captured? He had been what separated us from our parents. He had been our liberator. He played the background music while we grew up.

Elvis is dead. Suddenly, I didn't feel so good myself.

"Damn," said Price, "if Elvis is dead, that means we're getting old, too."

"Damn if it don't," said Franklin.

I asked for another beer.

The announcer on the radio had stopped talking, and the three of us fell silent as an eerie sound came forth. It was Elvis's voice. It was a dead man's voice. Elvis was singing "Don't Be Cruel." It was spooky.

" 'Don't Be Cruel'," said Price. "That was his best ever."

" 'One Night With You' was my favorite," Franklin said. "I remember dancing with Doris Ann Plummer and singing along with Elvis in her ear. 'Oooooooone ni-ite with yuuuuu is all I'm way-ayting fooor.' Doris Ann said I sounded just like Elvis, and soon as I got her in the car after the dance, it was all over."

"Everything he did was great," I said.

Elvis went on singing. I sat, still stupefied from the news, and listened. My friends went on talking.

"My old man hated Elvis."

"So did mine."

"He was always screaming at me, 'Get that garbage off the radio!'"

"Mine was a religious nut. He said the devil had sent Elvis, and anybody who listened to his music was going to hell."

"I wish my old man was alive today to see who the kids are idolizing now."

"Yeah, Elvis wouldn't look so bad compared to some of those weirdos they got today."

"He probably wouldn't even be noticed."

"You really scored with a girl because she thought you sounded like Elvis?"

"Doris Ann Plummer, right in the back seat out behind

the National Guard Armory."

"I always used Johnny Mathis."

"Well, Doris Ann wasn't exactly a great conquest. I found out later she'd do it if you sang like Lassie."

"Everybody had somebody like that in their school."

"Yeah, but just one."

"Imagine if it had been like it is now back then."

"I'd have never graduated from high school."

"I guess we were pretty naive back then compared to the kids now."

"Maybe we're better off."

"Maybe. I wonder if we'd have taken drugs if we'd had 'em back then."

"Hell, I thought drinking a beer was the wildest thing I could do."

"I went to a fraternity party at Auburn when I was a senior in high school. I drank gin and 7-Up and danced with college girls. I didn't think there was anything you could do any better or wilder than that."

"We didn't have it so bad growing up."

"At least we had Elvis."

"He was the greatest ever."

"The King."

"I don't think there will ever be anything like him again."

"Hard to believe he's dead."

"Think he was on drugs?"

"Probably."

"Ready for another beer?"

"Let's drink one to Elvis."

"To Elvis."

"To Elvis."

I joined in. "To Elvis."

The King was still singing on the radio:

"Love me tender,
Love me true,
Make all my dreams fulfilled.
For my darling, I love you.
And I always will."

* * *

I have never forgotten that day at the beach. It was like the day John Kennedy was killed. Like the day Martin Luther King was killed. Like the day Robert Kennedy was killed. Like the day Nixon resigned.

You never forget days like that, and you're never quite the same after them. There have been so many days like that, it seems, for my generation — the Baby Boomers who were minding to our business of growing up when all hell broke loose in the early sixties.

A few weeks after Elvis's death, I heard another piece of startling news. I heard they found Elvis dead in his bathroom. I heard he died straining for a bowel movement.

The King, we had called him, but he had gotten fat and at the age of forty-two he had died straining for a bowel movement. Or so was the rumor. I have spent much of the past seven years hoping against hope that it wasn't true.

8

When Life Was Black And White

I AM THIRTY-EIGHT years old — it's approximately half-time of the promised three score and ten — and I don't have any idea what is taking place around me anymore.

Lord knows, I have tried to understand. I have dutifully watched "Donahue" in an attempt to broaden myself into a creature adjusted to the eighties, but it has been a fruitless and frustrating endeavor.

How did Phil Donahue do it? He's even older than I am, with the gray hair to show for it, but he seems to understand what people mean when they talk about the new way to live. Me, I feel like an alien in my own country. These new lifestyles seem to be in direct contrast to the way they taught living when I was a child. Back then, *gay* meant, "1. Happy and carefree; merry. 2. Brightly colorful and ornamental. 3. Jaunty; sporty. 4. Full of or given to lighthearted pleasure. 5. Rakish; libertine." (That's straight from my high school dictionary.) Pot was something you cooked in, and back then nobody ate mushrooms. Where did I miss a

9

turn?

The first hint that the world was taking leave of me came after Elvis died. The women who mourned him were *older* and had beehive hairdos and children of their own. Their teeny-bopper, socks-rolled-down days were far behind them. They were my age and they were weeping not only for Elvis, I think now, but for the realization that an era and a time — their time — was passing to another generation. To know that Elvis had gotten old and sick and fat enough to die was to know that their own youth had faded as well.

Elvis, forty-two. Elvis, dead. The voice that sang for the children of the late forties and early fifties stilled, and in its place a cacophony of raucous melodies from scruffy characters playing to the screams of young earthlings of the modern generation, to whom happiness and normalcy was a computerized hamburger at McDonald's and mandatory attendance at earsplitting concerts given by people dressed as dragons or barely dressed at all. Elvis may have shaken his pelvis, but he never by-God showed it to anybody on stage.

Why this gap between me and the younger generation? Why, in my thirties, do I have more in common with people twenty years older than with people five or ten years younger? Where is my tolerance for change and modernization? Why would I enjoy hitting Boy George in the mouth? Where did the years go and where did the insanity of the eighties come from? And why did I ever leave home in the first place?

Home. That's probably it. I don't seem to fit in today because it was so different yesterday.

Home. I think of it and the way it was every time I see or hear something modern that challenges tradition as I came to know it.

10

Home. I was born in 1946, the son of a soldier who lived through seven years of combat and then drank his way right out of the service, but who still stood and sang the national anthem to the top of his forceful voice at the several hundred ball games we watched together.

Home. It was a broken home. That came when I was six and my mother ran for her parents and took me with her. The four of us lived in my grandparents' home. We warmed ourselves by kerosene, we ate from a bountiful garden, and our pattern of living was based on two books — the Bible and the Sears Roebuck catalog.

Everything came in black and white.

* * *

Moreland, Georgia, had perhaps three hundred inhabitants when I moved there in 1952. The population is about the same today, and Moreland still doesn't have a red light.

Some other things have changed, however. There are two tennis courts in Moreland. Back then, we played baseball and dammed creeks, and that was enough. Cureton and Cole's store, where the old men sat around the stove and spit and imparted wisdom, is boarded shut. I don't know where the old men in Moreland spit and impart wisdom nowadays.

Perhaps spitting and wisdom-imparting around a stove have gone the way of ice cream cups with pictures of movie stars on the bottom side of the lids. I purchased hundreds of ice cream cups at Cureton and Cole's, licking the faces of everybody from Andy Devine to Yvonne DeCarlo. I haven't seen ice cream cups like that in years, but even if they were still around, I wouldn't buy one; I'd be afraid I might lick away the vanilla on the bottom of my lid only to find John

11

Travolta smiling at me. What a horrid thought.

Those were good and honest people who raised me and taught me. They farmed, they worked in the hosiery mill that sat on the town square, and some went to the county seat six miles away where they welded and trimmed aluminum and sweated hourly-wage sweat — the kind that makes people hard and reserved and resolved there is a better world awaiting in the next life.

We had barbecues and street square dances in Moreland. We had two truckstops that were also beer joints, and the truckers played the pinball machines and the jukeboxes. The local beer drinkers parked their cars out back, presumably out of sight.

The religion in town was either Baptist or Methodist, and it was hardshell and certainly not tolerant of drinking. The church ladies were always gossiping about whose cars had been spotted behind the truckstops.

There was one fellow, however, who didn't care whether they saw his car or not. Pop Towns worked part-time at the post office, but the highlight of his day took place at the railroad yard. The train didn't stop in Moreland, so the outgoing mail had to be attached to a hook next to the tracks to be picked off when the train sped past. It was Pop's job to hang the mail.

Every morning at ten, when the northbound came through, and every evening at six, when the southbound passed, Pop would push his wheelbarrow filled with a sack of mail from the post office down to the tracks. There he would hang the mail, and we'd all stand around and watch as the train roared by. Then Pop would get in his car, drive over to one of the truckstops, park contemptuously out front, and have himself several beers.

12

One day the ladies of the church came to Pop's house in an effort to save him from the demon malt. I wasn't there when it happened, of course, but the word got around that when Pop answered the door for the ladies, he came with a beer in his hand.

Hilda Landon began reciting various scriptures regarding drunkenness. Pop countered by sicking his dog, Norman, on the ladies, and they scattered in various directions.

Pop, they said, laughed at the sight of his dog chasing off the ladies of the church, and once back inside his house, he had himself another beer, secure in the fact that he and Norman would never be bothered by another tolerance committee.

They found Pop dead one morning after he failed to make his appointment with the mail train, and the ladies of the church all said the Lord was getting even with Pop for all his sinful ways.

I sort of doubted that. Pop always had a good joke to tell and always was kind to his dog, and although I was no expert on the scriptures, I was of the belief that a good heart would get you a just reward in the afterlife as quick as anything else.

We also had a town drunk, Curtis "Fruit Jar" Hainey, but the ladies of the church figured he was too far gone to waste their efforts on. Curtis walked funny, like his knees were made of rubber. Somebody said it was because he once drank some rubbing alcohol when the local bootlegger left town for two weeks and Curtis came up dry and desperate. I figured the Lord could have had a little something to do with this one.

Although Moreland was a small town, not unlike so many others across the country in the early 1950s, we still had

13

plenty of scandal, intrigue, and entertainment.

It was whispered, for example, that Runelle Sheets, a high school girl who suddenly went to live with her cousin in Atlanta, actually was pregnant and had gone off to one of *those* homes.

Nobody ever verified the rumor about Runelle, but they said her daddy refused to speak her name in his house anymore and had threatened to kill a boy who lived over near Raymond. That was enough for a summer's full of satisfying speculation.

For further entertainment, we had a town idiot, Crazy Melvin, who allegedly was shell-shocked in Korea. Well, sort of. The story went that when Crazy Melvin heard the first shot fired, he began to run and when next seen had taken off his uniform, save his helmet and boots, and was perched in his nakedness in a small tree, refusing to climb down until frostbite threatened his privates.

They sent Crazy Melvin home after that, and following some months in the hospital, the Army decided that Melvin wasn't about to stop squatting naked in trees, so they released him in the custody of his parents.

Once back in Moreland, however, Crazy Melvin continued to do odd things, such as take off all his clothes, save his brogans and his straw hat. They finally sent Melvin to Atlanta to see a psychiatrist. When he came back, the psychiatrist had cured him of squatting naked in trees. Unfortunately, Melvin had ridden a trolley while in Atlanta and returned home thinking he was one. Every time you were walking to the store or to church and crossed paths with Crazy Melvin, you had to give him a nickel.

"Please step to the rear of the trolley," he would say, and then he'd make sounds like a trolley bell. The church later

14

got up enough money to buy Melvin one of those coin-holders bus drivers wear, so it was easier for him to make change when you didn't have a nickel.

* * *

Those were the days, when young boys roamed carefree and confidently around the streets of Moreland — Everytown, USA.

We were Baby Boomers all, born of patriots, honed by the traditional work ethic. That meant you worked your tail off and never quit until the job was done, and you saved every penny you could and never spent money on anything that didn't have at least some practical value. You kept the Word, never questioned authority, loved your country, did your duty, never forgot where you came from, bathed daily when there was plenty of water in the well, helped your neighbors, and were kind to little children, old people, and dogs. You never bought a car that was any color like red or yellow, stayed at home unless it was absolutely necessary to leave (such as going to church Sunday and for Wednesday night prayer meeting), kept your hair short and your face cleanshaven. You were suspicious of rich people, lawyers, yankee tourists, Catholics and Jehovah's Witnesses who tried to sell subscriptions to "The Watchtower" door-to-door, anybody who had a job where he had to wear a tie to work, and Republicans.

We were isolated in rural self-sufficiency for the most part. Television was only a rumor. We kept to ourselves unless we went to the county seat of Newnan to see a movie or to get a haircut or to see the little alligator they kept in a drink box at Mr. Lancaster's service station.

I never did find out how the little alligator got into a drink box at a service station in Newnan, Georgia, but rumor had it that Mr. Lancaster had brought it back from Florida to keep people from breaking into his station after he closed at night. In fact, Mr. Lancaster had a handwritten sign in front of his station that read, "This service station is guarded by my alligator three nights a week. Guess which three nights."

In such a closed, tightly-knit society, it was impossible not to feel a strong sense of belonging. Even for a newcomer.

When I first moved to Moreland at age seven, I was instantly befriended by the local boys. In those idyllic days, we molded friendships that would last for lifetimes.

There was Danny Thompson, who lived just across the cornfield from me, next door to Little Eddie Estes. Down the road from Danny was where Mike Murphy lived. Clyde and Worm Elrod lived near the Methodist Church. Bobby Entrekin and Dudley Stamps resided in Bexton, which was no town at all but simply a scattering of houses along a blacktop road a mile or so out of Moreland. There was Anthony Yeager, who lived over near Mr. Ralph Evans's store, and Charles Moore was just down the road from him.

Clyde Elrod was a couple of years older than his brother Worm, who was my age. Clyde had one ambition in his life, and that was to follow his father's footsteps into the Navy. Clyde often wore his father's old Navy clothes and regaled us with his father's Navy stories. Clyde's father apparently single-handedly won the battle for U.S. naval supremacy in World War II.

Worm got his name at Boy Scout camp one summer. There is only one thing worse than biting into an apple and finding a worm, and that's biting into an apple and finding half a worm, which is what happened to Worm Elrod and is how he got his nickname. Clyde and Worm did not get along that well, due to a heated sibling rivalry. Their father often had to separate them from various entanglements, and Worm invariably got the worst of it. Only when Clyde graduated from high school and left to join the Navy was it certain that Worm would live to see adulthood.

Anthony Yeager joined the gang later. He was the first of us to obtain his driver's license, and his popularity increased immediately. As teen-agers, we roamed in Yeager's Ford and slipped off for beer and to smoke. Once we went all the way to Fayetteville to the Highway 85 Drive-In and saw our first movie in which women appeared naked from the waist up.

Funny, what the memory recalls. The movie was *Bachelor Tom Peeping*, and it was billed as a documentary filmed at a nudist camp. At one point, Bachelor Tom was confronted by a huge-breasted woman who was covered only by a large inner tube that appeared to have come from the innards of a large tractor tire. As she lowered the tube, we watched in utter disbelief.

"Nice tubes you have, my dear," said Bachelor Tom.

Yeager was the first total devotee to country music I ever met, and he is at least partially responsible for my late-blooming interest in that sort of music. Yeager owned an old guitar that he couldn't play, but he tried anyway, and common were the nights we would find a quiet place in the woods, park his car, and serenade the surrounding critters.

17

Yeager's heroes were Hank Williams and Ernest Tubb. His favorite songs were Hank's "I'm So Lonesome I Could Cry" — later butchered by B.J. Thomas — and Ernest's classic, "I'm Walking the Floor Over You."

Hank was dead and long gone by then, but one day Yeager heard that Ernest Tubb, accompanied by picker-supreme Billy Byrd, was to perform at the high school auditorium in nearby Griffin. Me and Yeager and Dudley Stamps and Danny Thompson went. It was our first concert. Ernest slayed us, especially Yeager.

> *"I'm walkin' the floor over you.*
> *I can't sleep a wink, that is true.*
> *I'm hopin' and I'm prayin'*
> *That my heart won't break in two.*
> *I'm walkin' the floor over you."*

Whenever Ernest Tubb would call in Billy Byrd for a guitar interlude, he would say, "Awwwwwww, Billy Byrd," which Yeager thought was a nice touch. For months, Yeager would say "Awwwwwww, Billy Byrd" for no reason whatsoever. Later he began saying, "Put a feather in your butt and pick it out, Billy Byrd," again for no reason except that it seemed to give him great joy to say it.

Like I said, it's funny what details the memory recalls.

Dudley Stamps. He was the crazy one. He once drove his father's truck into White Oak Creek to see if trucks will float. They won't. There was not a water tower or a forest ranger tower in three counties he hadn't climbed. When he was old enough to get a driver's license, his parents bought him a used 1958 Thunderbird with a factory under the hood.

I was riding one night with Dudley when the State Patrol stopped him. His T-bird had been clocked at 110 MPH, according to the patrolman. Dudley was incensed and launched into an argument with the officer. He insisted he was doing at least 125.

Mike Murphy. He had a brother and sister and his father was called "Mr. Red." Mr. Red Murphy was the postmaster and helped with the Boy Scouts. With the possible exception of the Methodist and Baptist preachers, he was the most respected man in town. Mike had to work more than the rest of us. Mr. Red kept all his children busy tending the family acreage.

"You don't see Red Murphy's children out gallivantin' all over town," the old men around the stove used to say down at Cureton and Cole's. "Red keeps 'em in the fields where there ain't no trouble."

This was the late 1950s, when "gallivanting" meant doing just about anything that had no practical end to it, such as riding bicycles, roller-skating on the square, and hanging out at the store eating Zagnut candy bars and drinking NuGrapes or what was commonly referred to as "Big Orange bellywashers." Gallivanting, like most things modern, seems to have grown somewhat sterile and electronic. Today, I suppose when children gallivant it means they hang around in shopping malls, playing video games and eating frozen yogurt.

The day Mr. Red died was an awful day. It was the practice at the Moreland Methodist Church to return to the sanctuary after Sunday School for a quick hymn or two and for announcements by Sunday School Superintendent Fox Covin. Fox would also call on those having birthdays, and the celebrants would stand as we cheered them in song.

That Sunday morning, Fox Covin announced it was Mr. Red's birthday and asked his daughter to stand for him as we sang. As everyone in church knew, Mr. Red had been hospitalized the day before for what was alleged to be a minor problem.

Soon after we sang to Mr. Red, another member of the family came into the church and whisked the Murphy children away. Something was whispered to Fox Covin, and after the children were safely out of earshot, he told the congregation that Red Murphy was dead.

We cried and then we prayed. Mike was no more than twelve or thirteen at the time. He had to take on a great deal of the responsibility of the farm after that, so his opportunity to gallivant with the rest of us was shortened even further.

"Mike Murphy will grow up to be a fine man," my mother used to say.

Bobby Entrekin. I loved his father. I had secretly wished there was some way my mother could have married Mr. Bob Entrekin, but there was his wife, Miss Willie, with whom to contend, and a quiet, soft, loving woman she was. I decided to remain content with spending my weekends at the Entrekin home.

Mr. Bob worked nights. Miss Willie worked days at one of the grocery stores in the county seat. The Entrekins, I noticed, ate better than the rest of us. While my family's diet consisted mostly of what we grew from our garden or raised in our chicken coops, the Entrekins always had such delights as store-bought sandwich meat and boxed dough-nuts, the sort with the sweet, white powder around them.

The standing contention was that because Miss Willie was employed at the grocery store, she was given discounts on such elaborate foodstuffs others in the community would have found terribly wasteful to purchase.

Whatever, as much as I enjoyed the company of my friend Bobby Entrekin, it may have been the lure of the delights of his family refrigerator and his father that were the most binding seal on our friendship.

Bobby's father was unlike any man I had ever met before. He had a deep, forceful voice. His knowledge of sport was unparalleled in the community. He had once been an out-standing amateur baseball player, and on autumn Satur-days, Bobby and I would join him at radioside to listen to Southeastern Conference college football games — as com-forting and delicious an exercise as I have ever known. My own father, having split for parts unknown, had shared Mr. Bob's affinity for sports and other such manly interests, and Mr. Bob stood in for him nicely.

Mr. Bob also had more dimension to him than any other man I had known. He had educated himself. He had trav-eled a bit. He sent off for classical records, and when I spent the weekends with Bobby, his father would awaken us on Sunday mornings for church with those foreign sounds.

As Beethoven roared through the little Entrekin house out on Bexton Road, he would say to us, "Boys, that is what you call good music." How uncharacteristic of the time and place from which I sprung, but how pleasant the memory.

Bobby was a con man from his earliest days. He slicked classmates out of their lunch desserts, and by schoolday's end, he usually had increased his marble holdings considerably.

Only once did he put an unpleasant shuck on me. Mr. Bob had driven us into Newnan, where the nearest picture show was located. The Alamo Theatre sat on Newnan's court square, across the street from the side entrance to the county courthouse. Admission to the movie was a dime. There were soft drinks for a nickel and small bags of popcorn for the same price.

As we walked toward the Alamo, we came upon a bus parked on the court square.

"Boys," said a man sitting outside the bus, "come on inside and see the world's fattest woman."

"How fat is she?" Bobby asked.

"Find out for yourself for only fifteen cents, kid," said the man.

Bobby started inside while I did some quick arithmetic. I had twenty cents. That was a dime for admission to the picture show and a dime for a soft drink and popcorn. If I paid fifteen cents to see the fat lady, I couldn't get in to see the movie.

I mentioned this bit of financial difficulty to Bobby.

"Don't worry," he said. "I'll loan you enough to get into the show."

We each dropped fifteen cents into the man's cigar box of coins and stepped inside the bus.

The smell got us first. A hog would have buried its snout in the mud to have escaped it. Then we saw the fat lady. She was enormous. She dripped fat. She was laid out on a divan, attempting to fan away the heat and the stench. We both ran out of the bus toward the movie house.

When we arrived at the ticket window, I reminded Bobby

of his offer to stake me to a ticket.

"I was only kidding," he said, as he pranced into the theater. I sat on the curb and cried. Later, when I told his father what Bobby had done, Mr. Bob played a symphony upon his son's rear and allowed me to watch. I took shameful pleasure in the sweet revenge.

Charles Moore. His mother called him "Cholly," and he eventually achieved some renown in high school when The Beatles hit in 1964 because Charles, even with his short hair, was a dead-ringer for a seventeen-year-old Paul McCartney. Charles was never able to make any money off this resemblance — that was before the imitation craze, e.g., the Elvis impersonators after his death and the three or four thousand young black kids currently doing Michael Jackson — but he obviously took a great deal of pleasure from standing in the middle of a group of giggling girls who were saying things like, "Oh, Charles, you look just like Paul."

What I remember Charles for most, however, is the fight we had in the seventh grade over a baseball score. I was a fierce and loyal Dodger fan. Charles held the same allegiance to the Milwaukee Braves.

I arrived at school one morning with a score from the evening before, Dodgers over the Braves. I had heard it on the radio.

"The Dodgers beat the Braves last night," I boasted to Charles.

"No they didn't," he said.

"I heard it on the radio," I continued.

"I don't care what you heard," he said. "The Braves won."

The principal had to pull us apart.

When I went home that afternoon, I called Mr. Bob Entrekin, who subscribed to the afternoon paper with the complete scores, and asked him to verify the fact that the Dodgers had, indeed, defeated the Braves so I could call Charles Moore and instruct him to kiss my tail.

The Braves had won, said Mr. Bob. I feigned a sore throat and didn't go to school the next two days.

Danny Thompson. We were best friends before high school. Danny was the best athlete in our class. At the countywide field day competition, he ran fourth in the potato race. A potato race works — or worked, since I doubt potato racing has lingered with everybody throwing those silly frisbees today — this way:

There were four cans (the kind that large quantities of mustard and canned peaches came in) spaced at intervals of ten yards. The boy running first can dashed the first ten yards, picked the potato out of the can, and raced back and handed it to the boy running second can.

He then dropped the potato into the team can at the starting line and hurried to the second can twenty yards away. The team that got all four potatoes in its can first won the medals.

Danny ran fourth can because he was the fastest boy in our class. We probably would have won the county potato race, had I not stumbled and dropped my potato as I tried to depart from the second can.

Danny was also rather possessive about his belongings. He received a new football for Christmas one year. It was a Sammy Baugh model, and it had white stripes around each end. We were perhaps ten when Danny got the football.

24

We gathered for a game of touch a few days after Christmas, but Danny didn't bring his new football.

"I'm saving it," he explained.

When I would visit Danny, he would pull his new football out of his closet and allow me to hold it. He would never take it outside, however.

"I'm saving it," he would say again. That was nearly thirty years ago. We never did get to play with Danny's football.

One morning in the fifth grade, I looked over at Danny and his face was in his hands. He was crying. I had never seen Danny cry before. The teacher whispered something to him and then took him out of the room.

Word travels fast in a small town. Danny's mother and his father had separated. He and I were even closer in our friendship after that. We shared a loss of parent uncommon to children then, but we rolled quite well with our punch, I suppose. We spent hours together deep down in the woods behind his house. He talked of his mother. I talked of my father.

Danny wanted us to become blood brothers. He had seen two Indians on television cut their fingers and then allow their blood to mix. I wanted to be Danny's blood brother, but I was afraid to cut my finger. I suggested that we swap comic books instead.

* * *

It was a simple childhood, one that I didn't fully cherish until I had long grown out of it. Only then did I appreciate the fact that I was allowed to grow into manhood having never once spent a day at the country club pool, or playing baseball where they put the ball on a tee like they do for children today, or growing my hair down over my shoulders, or wearing T-shirts advertising punk rock bands, or smoking anything stronger than a rabbit tobacco cigarette wrapped in paper torn from a brown bag and, later, an occasional Marlboro Dudley Stamps would bring on camping trips from his father's store.

It was a most happy childhood, because the only real fear we had was that we might somehow find ourselves at odds with Frankie Garfield. Frankie was the town bully who often made life miserable for all of us, especially any new child who moved into Moreland. There was the new kid with the harelip, for instance.

The afternoon of his first day in school, the new kid rode his bicycle to Cureton and Cole's, where Frankie was involved in beating up a couple of fifth graders for their NuGrapes and Zagnut candy bars.

The new kid parked his bicycle, and as he walked to the entrance of the store, he reached down to pick up a shiny nail off the ground. Frankie spotted him.

"Hey, Harelip," he called, "that's my nail."

Nobody had bothered to inform the new kid about Frankie Garfield. The rest of us knew that if Frankie said the nail was his, the best move was to drop the nail immediately, apologize profusely, and then offer to buy Frankie anything inside the store he desired.

The new kid, however, made a serious, nearly fatal, mistake. He indicated, in no uncertain terms, that Frankie was filled with a rather unpleasant substance common to barnyards. Then he put the nail in his pocket and began to walk inside the store.

He didn't make it past the first step before Frankie began to beat him unmercifully. At first, I think Frankie was sim-

26

ply amusing himself, as a dog amuses himself by catching a turtle in his mouth and slinging it around in the air.

Then the new kid made another mistake. He tried to fight back against Frankie. Now Frankie was mad. When he finally tired of beating his victim, Frankie left him there in a crumpled heap and rode off on the new kid's bicycle.

I suppose Frankie did have some degree of heart about him. He let the new kid keep the nail.

We were involved in some occasional juvenile delinquency, but nothing more flagrant than stealing a few watermelons, or shooting out windows in abandoned houses, or pilfering a few peaches over at Cates's fruit stand.

We went to church, didn't talk back to our elders, studied history in which America never lost a war, and were basically what our parents wanted us to be. Except when it came to Elvis.

* * *

Whatever else we were, we were the first children of television, and it was television that brought us Elvis. He would prove to be the first break between our parents and ourselves. That disagreement seems so mild today after the generational war that broke out in the late sixties, but those were more timid times when naiveté was still in flower.

Elvis was a Pied Piper wearing ducktails. He sang and he moaned and wiggled, and we followed him ... taking our first frightening steps of independence.

Guilt
Trip
In A
Cadillac

RADIO PERHAPS WOULD have made Elvis popular, but television made him The King. We could *see* him, and there never had been anything like him before.

The only music I knew prior to Elvis was the hymns from the Methodist Cokesbury hymnal; "My Bucket's Got a Hole in It" and "Good Night, Irene" from my mother's singing while she ironed; and "Peace in the Valley," which I had learned watching "The Red Foley Show" on Saturday nights after my aunt bought the first television in the family.

But Elvis. Ducktails. His guitar. Uh-uh, Baby, don't you step on my blue suede shoes, and don't be cruel to a heart that's true.

Elvis thrust a rebellious mood upon us. I was ten or eleven when I decided to grow my own ducktails and refused to get my little-boy flattop renewed. As my hair grew out, I pushed back the sides by greasing them down, and then I brought my hair together at the back of my head, giving it the appearance of the north end of a southbound duck. I

28

wouldn't wash my hair, either, for fear it might lose what I considered to be a perfect set.

"If you don't wash your hair, young man," my mother would warn me, "you're going to get head lice."

I didn't believe her. Nothing, not even head lice, could live in that much greasy gook.

I also pushed my pants down low like Elvis wore his.

"Pull your pants up before they fall off," my mother would say.

"This is how Elvis wears his pants," would be my inevitable reply.

"I don't know what you children see in him," she would counter.

I wrote her off as completely without musical taste and suggested that Red Foley was an incompetent old geezer who couldn't carry Elvis's pick.

"I don't know what's wrong with young'uns these days," was my mother's subsequent lament.

My stepfather eventually entered the ducktail disagreement and dragged me to the barber to reinstate my shorn looks. I cried and pouted and refused to come to the dinner table. Why were these people so insistent that I maintain the status quo when there was something new out there to behold?

We fought the Elvis battle in my house daily. Sample warfare:

"How can you stand that singing?"

"Elvis is a great singer."

"Sounds like a lot of hollering and screaming to me."

"It's rock 'n' roll."

"It's garbage."

"It's Elvis."

"It's garbage."

"It is not."

"Don't you talk back to me, young man!"

"I wasn't talking back."

"You're talking back now."

"I am not."

"Turn off that music right now and go to bed. This Elvis is ruining all our children."

I suppose if it hadn't been Elvis who ruined us, it would have been something, or somebody, else. But it *was* Elvis, and it was his music that set us off on a course different from that of our parents.

"That Elvis," the old men around the stove at Cureton and Cole's would say, "ain't nothin' but a white nigger."

"Don't sing nothin' but nigger music."

"That little ol' gal of mine got to watchin' him on the teevee and he started all that movin' around like he does — look like a damn dog tryin' to hump on the back of a bitch in heat — and I made her shet him off. Ought not allow such as that on the teevee."

"Preacher preached on him last week. Said he was trash and his music was trash."

"He's ruinin' the young'uns."

The teachers at Moreland School caught one of the Turnipseed boys, I think it was Bobby Gene, shaking and humping like Elvis to the delight of a group of fifth-grade girls on the playground one morning during recess.

They took him to the principal, who paddled him and sent a note home to his parents, explaining his lewd behavior. Bobby Gene's daddy whipped him again.

"Do your Elvis for us, Bobby Gene," we said when he came back to school.

30

"Can't," he replied. "I'm too sore."

Bobby Gene Turnipseed may have done the best Elvis impersonation in Moreland, but each of Elvis's male followers had his own version. After my stepfather forced me to have my ducktails sheared back into a flattop, my Elvis lost a little something, but I still prided myself on the ability to lift the right side of my lip, à la Elvis's half-smile, half-snarl that sent the girls into fits of screaming and hand-clutching.

There was a girl in my Sunday School class who was a desirable young thing, and as our Sunday School teacher read our lesson one morning, I decided to do my Elvis half-smile, half-snarl for the latest object of my ardor.

Recall that we were children of church-minded people, and I was quite aware of the wages of sin. I once snitched a grape at Cureton and Cole's, and my cousin saw me and told me I was going to hell for thievery. I was so disturbed that I went back to the store and confessed my crime to Mr. J.W. Thompson, one of the owners. He was so moved by my admission of guilt that he gave me an entire sack of grapes free and assured me I'd have to steal a car or somebody's dog to qualify for eternal damnation. When my cousin asked me to share my grapes with her, I told her to go to.... Well, I ate all the grapes myself and spit the seeds at her.

Stealing grapes was one thing, but thinking unspeakable thoughts about girls while in church and curling my lip at my prepubescent Cleopatra while the lesson was being read probably would bring harsh punishment from above. I couldn't remember which thou-shalt-not such activity fell under — I wasn't certain what *covet* meant, but I figured it had something to do with wanting another boy's bicycle — so I decided to take a chance and do my Elvis lip trick at the

31

girl anyway.

I curled up the right side of my lip perfectly as Cleo looked over at me. I didn't know what to expect. Would she absolutely *melt?* Would she want to meet me after church and go over to what was left of the abandoned cotton gin and give me kisses and squeezes?

She didn't do either. What she did was tell the Sunday School teacher I was making weird faces at her while the lesson was being read. The teacher told my mother about it, and my punishment was to read the entire book of Deuteronomy and present a report on it to the class the next Sunday. I learned a valuable lesson from all that: When you're in church, keep your mind on baseball or what you're going to have for lunch, not on something sweet and soft and perfumed wearing a sundress. Church and Evening in Paris simply don't mix.

Never one to be selfish, I attempted to share my ability to mime Elvis's facial expressions with others, especially with Little Eddie Estes. Little Eddie was a couple of years younger than me and I served as his self-appointed mentor. I taught him how to bunt, where to look in the Sears Roebuck catalog for the most scintillating pictures of women in their underpants, how to tell if a watermelon is ripe (you cut out a plug and if what you see inside is red, it's ripe), and I also attempted to instruct him in mimicking Elvis.

"What you do is this," I said to Little Eddie. "You curl your lip to the right a little bit, like the dog just did something smelly. If you want to add Elvis's movements to this, you bring one leg around like a wasp has crawled inside your pants leg, and then you move the other and groan like when your mother insists you eat boiled cabbage."

32

Little Eddie made a gallant attempt. He got the lip fine and he groaned perfectly, but he couldn't get the legs to shake in the correct manner.

"I couldn't shake my legs, either, when I first started doing Elvis," I told him. "What you need to do is practice in front of a mirror."

Several days later, Little Eddie's father found his son curling his lip and groaning and shaking his legs in front of a mirror in his bedroom and thought he was having some sort of seizure. His mother gave him a dose of Castor Oil and put him to bed.

* * *

I don't suppose that any generation has really understood the next, and every generation has steadfastly insisted that the younger adapt its particular values and views.

My parents' generation, true to form, sought to bring up its young in its mold, but it also had a firm resolve to do something more for us.

It was much later in my life, perhaps at a time I was feeling terribly sorry for myself and looking for a way out of that constant dilemma, that I decided my parents' generation may have endured more hardship and offered more sacrifices than any other previous generation of Americans.

So they never had to cross the Rockies in covered wagons and worry about being scalped. But my parents, both of whom were born in 1912, would live through and be directly affected by two World Wars, one Great Depression, and whatever you call Korea. And when they had been through all that, they were ushered into the Cold War and had to decide whether or not to build a fallout shelter.

It is no wonder that the men and women who came from those harried times were patriots, were traditionalists, were believers in the idea that he who worked and practiced thrift prospered, and he who allowed the sun to catch him sleeping and was wasteful perished.

These were hard people, who had lived through hard times. But they endured and the country endured, and they came away from their experiences with a deep belief in a system that had been tested but had emerged with glorious victory.

Looking back on my relationship with my own parents and with others from their generation, I think they also felt a sense of duty to their children to make certain that, at whatever cost, their children would be spared the adversity they had seen.

Have we, the Baby Boomers, not heard our parents say a thousand times, "We want you to have it better than we did"?

They wanted to protect us. They wanted to educate us. They wanted us to be doctors and lawyers and stockbrokers, not farmers and mill hands. They hounded us to study and to strive and avoid winding up in a job that paid an hourly wage. They may have mistrusted individuals their own age who had educations and who went to work wearing ties, but that's exactly what they wanted for us. And they made us feel terribly guilty if we did not share their desires.

"Have you done your homework?" my mother would ask.

"I'll do it later."

"You will do it now, young man. I don't want you winding up on the third shift at Flagg-Utica."

Flagg-Utica was a local textile plant.

"I haven't bought anything new to wear in years so I could save for your education," my mother would continue on her

34

guilt trip, "and you don't have the gratitude to do your homework."

Somehow, I never could figure how failing to read three chapters in my geography book about the various sorts of vegetation to be found in a tropical rain forest had anything to do with facing a life as a mill hand. But with enough guilt as a catalyst, you can read anything, even geography books and Deuteronomy.

I suppose our parents also were trying to protect us when they voiced their displeasure with Elvis. They knew he was something different, too, and they were afraid of where he might lead — thinking evil thoughts about girls in Sunday School, for example.

We want you to have it better than we did, they said, and that covered just about everything. They wanted us to have money and comforts; they wanted us to have knowledge and vision; they wanted a better world for us, one free from war and bitter sacrifice.

They are old now, my parents' generation, and I suppose they think they got what they wanted. I did my homework and I got the education my mother saved for, and I live in an air-conditioned house with a microwave oven, an automatic ice-maker, and a Jenn-Air grill on the stove. I also have two color television sets with remote control, a pair of Gucci loafers, and a tennis racquet that cost more than the 1947 Chevrolet my mother once bought. I eat steak whenever I want it, I've been to Europe a couple of times and nobody shot at me, and I have a nice car.

The car. It's a perfect manifestation of having achieved the success my parents wanted for me, but such success can be bittersweet. While we're having it better than our parents did, they now may feel, in some instances, that we've actually

35

gone further than they intended. They may suspect, as the phrase went, that we've forgotten "where we came from."

Allow me to explain.

After I got my first job out of college, I bought myself a Pontiac. Later, I bought another Pontiac, bigger and with more features than the previous one. Then I lost my head and bought one of those British roadsters that was approximately the size of a bumper car at the amusement park but not built nearly as solidly.

After the sports car had driven me sufficiently nuts, I decided to go back to a full-sized sedan, something fitting a person who was having it better than his parents did.

I got myself a Cadillac.

Nobody in my family had ever owned a Cadillac, so I figured if I had one, there could be no question that I had fulfilled my mother's wishes by making something of myself.

I had a former schoolmate who sold Cadillacs, so I went to see him and priced a couple. I couldn't have paid for the back seat, much less an entire Cadillac.

"Have you thought about leasing?" my friend asked me.

As a matter of fact, I hadn't. As a matter of fact, I never had even heard of leasing an automobile.

"It's the latest thing," said my friend, who explained that I wouldn't have to fork over any huge down payment, and for a modest (by Arab oil sheik standards) monthly installment, I could be driving around in a brand-new Cadillac.

I bit.

"You want power steering and power brakes, of course," said my friend.

"Of course."

"And do you want leather upholstery?"

36

"Of course."

"And how about wire wheelcovers and a sun roof?"

"Of course."

"And eight-track stereo?"

"Of course."

"Let me see if I have this straight," my friend summarized. "You want the kind of Cadillac that if you drove it home to Moreland and parked it in your mother's yard, half the town would want to come by and see it. Right?"

"But, of course," I said.

I drove my new Cadillac with the power steering and the power brakes and the leather upholstery and the wire wheelcovers and the eight-track stereo off the lot and directly home to Moreland.

"It must have been expensive," said my mother.

"Not really," I explained. "I leased it."

"Couldn't you have done just as well with a Chevrolet? I always had good luck with Chevrolets."

"I just thought it was time I got myself a Cadillac," I explained. "I've worked hard."

"I know that, son," said my mother, "but I don't want you just throwing your money away on fancy cars."

Suddenly, I felt guilty for driving up in my mother's yard in a Cadillac. I was feeling guilty because I didn't think a Chevrolet was good enough for me anymore. I could hear the old men sitting around the stove:

"Got yourself a Cadillac, huh? Boy, ain't you big-time?"

"Hey, look who got hisself a Cadillac, ol' college-boy here. Boy, where'd you learn high-falootin' things like drivin' a Cadillac? Didn't learn that from your mama, I know that. She never drove nothing but Chevrolets."

The only person who came by to see my car while I was

37

visiting my mother was Crazy Melvin.

"What kind of car is it?" he asked me.

"Chevrolet," I said.

"Thought so," said Crazy Melvin as he walked away.

Guilt was a very big part of my generation's adult life. If you didn't do well enough, you were guilty because you'd let your parents down. But if you did too well, and came home driving a Cadillac and wearing sunglasses, you felt guilty because you obviously had forgotten your roots and had turned into a big-city high-roller that you had no business turning into.

The old men at the store: "You drivin' that Cadillac is like puttin' a ten dollar saddle on a thousand dollar horse."

Despite the Cadillac, which now has more than 100,000 miles on it and is five years old (I figure if I drive it long enough, my mother will appreciate the sound common sense I used in not trading for a new car until my old one was completely worn out), despite the education, despite all the gadgetry I own, despite the fact that I didn't wind up on the third shift at Flagg-Utica, I'm not so certain that I *am* having it better than my parents' generation did.

Let me clarify this point: I wouldn't have wanted to go through World Wars and the Great Depression, and I like my creature comforts and the cruise control on my car, but did my parents ever have to eat a plastic breakfast at McDonald's while some guy mopped under their table spreading the aroma of ammonia?

Did they ever have to fight five o'clock traffic on a freeway when they were my age? Did they ever have to worry about getting herpes? Couldn't they eat bacon and all those other foods that are supposed to give me everything from St. Vitus Dance to cancer without worrying?

38

Did they ever have to put up with calling somebody and getting a recorded message? Did they ever have to make their own salads in restaurants or pump their own gasoline at exorbitant prices in gasoline stations? Didn't they get free glasses when they bought gas, and didn't the attendant always wash their windshield and check their oil without being asked?

Did my parents' generation go to movies and not understand them at all? Did they ever have to deal with women's liberation, gay rights, the Moral Majority, the anti-nuke movement, a dozen kinds of racism, palimony, sex discrimination suits, and Phil Donahue making you wonder if you really have any business on this planet anymore?

Did they have to endure Valley Girls, punk rock, rock videos, the "moonwalk," break dancing, ghetto blasters, and "The Catlins"?

So their kids worshipped Elvis. My generation's children follow Michael Jackson, who wears one glove and his sunglasses at night, and sings songs with names like "Beat It." It also is rumored that he takes female hormones to nullify his voice change. I cannot verify this, but there are rumors he recently was seen hanging his panty hose on a shower rod. My generation's children also follow something called "Culture Club," which features something called Boy George, who dresses like Zasu Pitts.

My parents' generation had Roosevelt for a president. We had Nixon.

They won their war. We lost ours.

They knew exactly what their roles in family and society were. Most of us don't have any idea what ours are anymore.

They had corns on their toes. We have identity crises.

They got married first and then lived together. We do it

39

just the opposite today.

They fell in love. We fall, or try to, into meaningful relationships.

Did Lou Gehrig use cocaine? Did Jack Benny freebase? Did Barbara Stanwyck get naked on the silver screen? Did they have to put up with Jane Fonda?

I obviously can't speak for all of us, but here is one Baby Boomer who liked it better when it was simpler. My parents sent me out into this world to make for myself a better life than they had and maybe I achieved that in some way. But the everlasting dilemma facing me is that although I live in a new world, I was reared to live in the old one.

I remain the patriot they taught me to be. I like music you can whistle to. If ever I marry again, it will have to be to a woman who will cook. She can be a lawyer or work construction in the daytime, and she can have her own bank account and wear a coat and tie for all I care, but I want a home-cooked meal occasionally where absolutely nothing has passed through a microwave.

I don't understand the gay movement. I don't care if you make love to Nash Ramblers, as long as you're discreet about it.

I don't use drugs, and I don't understand why anybody else does as long as there's cold beer around.

I think computers are dangerous, men who wear earrings are weird, the last thing that was any good on television was "The Andy Griffith Show," and I never thought Phyllis George had any business talking about football with Brent Musberger on television.

In his classic song, "Are the Good Times Really Over for Good?", Merle Haggard says it best:

"Wish Coke was still cola,
A joint, a bad place to be ...
It was back before Nixon lied to us all on TV ...
Before microwave ovens, when a girl could still cook and still
would ...
Is the best of the free life behind us now,
Are the good times really over for good?"

My sentiments exactly. If I could have the good times back, I would bring back 1962. At least, most of it. I was sixteen then. I had my driver's license, a blonde girlfriend, and my mother awakened me in the mornings and fed me at night.

Elvis was still singing, Kennedy was still president, Sandy Koufax was still pitching, John Wayne was still acting, Arnold Palmer was still winning golf tournaments, you could still get hand-cut french fries in restaurants, there was no such thing as acid rain or Three Mile Island, men got their hair cut in barber shops and women got theirs cut at beauty parlors, there was no such person as Calvin Klein, nobody used the word *psychedelic,* nobody had ever heard of Vietnam, and when nobody bombed anybody during the Cuban Missile Crisis, I was convinced that the world was probably safe from nuclear annihilation ... an idea I do not hold to with much force anymore.

1962. It was a beauty.

So what happened to the simple life the boys from Moreland knew? And when did all the change begin?

I think I can answer the second question. It was one morning in November, 1963, and I was changing classes in high school.

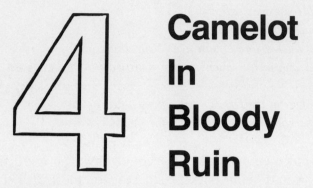

4 Camelot In Bloody Ruin

L ET THE WORD go forth from this time and place... that the torch has been passed to a new generation of Americans...."
John F. Kennedy, January 20, 1961

There was one family of Catholics in Moreland in 1960. They had to drive ten miles to the county seat to go to church. I didn't think there was anything particularly different about them except that on Fridays, when the rest of us were attempting to force down what they said was meatloaf but tasted like Alpo looks, the kids from the Catholic family were eating what appeared to be a tasty serving of fried fish. Had it not been for the fact that it would have put the good Methodists and Baptists in my family into shock and running fits, I might have become a Catholic, too, just to avoid the Friday meatloaf.

The adults in town didn't trust Catholics. One of the old men down at the store said he heard they stole babies. Somebody else said Catholics drank a lot, and half the time they didn't even speak English when they were holding church services.

John Kennedy frightened the local voting bloc, perhaps a hundred-or-so strong. He was Catholic and his daddy was rich, and despite the fact we're talking lifelong Democrats here, they were having a difficult time accepting the idea that a person with religious beliefs so foreign to their own might actually occupy the White House.

The old men around the stove:

"I ain't sure we ought to elect no Cathlic."

"I ain't votin' for him. He'd take all his orders from the Vaddican."

"The what?"

"The Vaddican."

"Where's that?"

"Itly."

"Reckon that's so?"

"'Course it's so. Them Cathlics stick together like buttermilk sticks to your chin."

"You ever know'd any Cathlics?"

"Naw, but I think one come in the truckstop a week or so ago."

"How'd you know it was a Cathlic?"

"He's wearing a white shirt. Who else 'round here wears white shirts?"

If Elvis was the first break between the Baby Boomers and their parents, then John Kennedy — at least in rural Georgia, which was my only horizon at the time — was a second. Kennedy never started the youthful explosion that Elvis had, but there was something about the man that appealed to us. It was later described as "vigah." Although I was too young to vote in the 1960 presidential election, I did my part to elect Kennedy by running down Richard Nixon.

I was born under Truman and then came Ike. The General was okay, but I didn't like the way Nixon, his vice president for eight years, looked even then. He already had those jowls, and when he talked, it seemed like his mouth was full of spit and he needed to swallow.

I also was never able to understand how Nixon fathered any children, because I was convinced he slept in his suit. I suspect Richard Nixon was born wearing a tiny little suit and tie, and his aunts and uncles probably stood around his crib and looked at his beady little eyes and at his jowls — I'm sure he was born with them, too — and said things like, "Well, let's hope and pray he grows out of it."

He didn't, of course. The older he got, the shiftier he looked, and that's why Kennedy beat him in 1960. When they debated, Nixon looked like a 1952 Ford with a busted tailpipe and foam rubber dice hanging off his rear-view mirror; Kennedy was a Rolls Royce in comparison.

All the girls at school liked Kennedy, too. "He's sooo cute," was their usual adept analysis of his platform.

Historians who have looked back on the brief thousand days that John Kennedy was our president have failed to note that Kennedy did, in fact, accomplish an important feat with his looks. Remember his hair? John Kennedy's hair was sort of fluffy. Nixon probably greased his down with whatever it was I used to slick down my ducktails.

In the early 1960s, most men were still using Vitalis and Wildroot Creme Oil on their hair. But I don't think John Kennedy used anything like that on his. In fact, Kennedy may have been the first American male to show off "The Dry Look." It was only a few years after Kennedy became president that we celebrated the death of "The Wethead," and American men poured their hair tonic down the drain and spent millions on blow-dryers and hairspray.

Looks are important to a president, and Kennedy was the most handsome American president since Andrew Jackson — who wasn't any Tom Selleck, but at least he didn't have one of those cherub-looking faces like John Quincy Adams, and he didn't wear a powdered wig.

Look at the appearances of our presidents over the years. The pictures of George Washington that were in our history books made the father of our country look like somebody's sweet little grandmother. Abraham Lincoln was no day at the beach, either, and Rutherford B. Hayes had that long scraggly beard, and William Taft was fat. FDR was fairly handsome, but he used that long cigarette holder that made him appear a bit stuffy, I thought. Truman wore funny hats and bow ties, and Eisenhower was militarily rigid and grandfatherly.

John Kennedy, however, *was* the torchbearer for the new generation. If the times were Camelot, then he was certainly Arthur. He seemed more of an admired, understanding big brother to us than an awesome patriarch ruling from some distant perch.

The youth of the early sixties knew little of the system, other than what we had learned in Civics class, but here was a man with whom we were able to relate — if not to his substance, then most certainly to his style.

The Cuban Missile Crisis brought us even closer to him. He told the Russians where he wanted them to stick their missiles and in the meantime created several marvelously exciting days at my high school. I didn't pay a great deal of attention to the crisis at first. Basketball practice had started, and that had me too occupied to consider the end of the world as we knew it.

I was in Jacobs's Drug Store in Newnan eating a banana split the night the president went on television in October of 1962 and told the nation that we were about this far from having to sink a few Russian ships and maybe start World War III. I hesitated and watched and listened for a few moments, but then I went back to the banana split.

The next day at school, however, our principal, Mr. O.P. Evans, called the student body together and began to prepare us for the nuclear attack he seemed certain would come before the noon lunch bell.

Mr. Evans was a tall, forceful man with a deep, booming voice that was a fearful and commanding thing. He ran the school with a Bible in one hand and a paddle in the other. The school was his passion, and even an imminent nuclear attack would not deter him from making certain that we would be a model of order until the last one of us had been melted into a nuclear ash.

We were told that when (I don't think he ever mentioned an "if" anywhere) the call came to Mr. Evans's office (probably directly from Washington) to inform him that the bombs and missiles were on the way, we would be hastened back to assembly for further instructions. At that point, a decision would be made on whether or not to close school and send us home. In the event we could not safely evacuate, we would remain at school and be given subsequent assignments as to where we would bed down for the night.

That idea caused a great stirring of interest among the boys. Would we get to sleep near the girls? Could we slip around and perhaps catch them in nothing but their underpants? Bring on the bombs and missiles. Mr. Evans quickly dashed our hopes, however, by stating that the boys would

46

be herded to the gymnasium, while the girls would sleep at the other end of the school in the cafeteria and the student activities room, where the Coke and candy machines were also located, damn the luck.

He instructed us to bring canned goods to store in our lockers the following day, presuming there was one, in case the school ran out of food and we had to spend the winter inside the building waiting for the fallout to subside. Students also were to bring blankets and soap, an extra toothbrush, and a change of clothes and underwear. The sacks of clothes and underwear were stored on the stage in the assembly room. Having been shut out of actually getting to see our female classmates down to their skivvies, a group of us went for the next best thing and sneaked into the assembly room during the post-lunch rest period and went through the sacks trying to match girls with panties and bras.

The possibility of an attack did lose some of its glamour, however, when Mr. Evans further announced that as long as a single teacher survived, classes would continue and gum chewing would remain a capital offense.

The attack never came, of course, but we did find out that Gayle Spangler, who always was going off to Atlanta on weekends and was allegedly keeping company with college boys and going to wild fraternity parties, had a pair of panties with the 1962 Georgia Tech football schedule printed on the crotch.

John Kennedy was hailed as a conqueror after backing down the Russians and their missiles, but the triumphant mood of the country was short-lived. One moment Camelot was there, and the next it lay in bloody ruin.

It was the autumn of my senior year. November, 1963. I

47

was changing morning classes. I had just finished Spanish, which I hated. I particularly hated those silly records they played to us in Spanish class.

"El burro es un animal de Mexico, Espana, y Norte Americana, tambien. Repeata, por favor."

Thirty students with heavy Southern accents would repeat: "El boorow ez uhn anymahl de Mexeecoh, Espainya, why Gnawertee Amuricainya, tambiann."

I was strolling down the hallway toward geometry class. Something was happening. The teachers had come out into the hall and were herding students into classrooms.

"Don't go to your next class. Come into my room. Quickly," said a teacher to me.

The halls were cleared. There was an eerie silence. Is the place on fire? Have the Russians decided to attack after all? Has somebody been caught chewing gum? I noticed the teacher sitting in the desk in front of me. She was holding back tears.

The voice. I had heard that powerful voice so many times, but now it seemed to crack and strain.

"Your attention, please," said Mr. Evans over the intercom. "We have just received word that President John Kennedy has been shot in Dallas. We have no other word at this time. May we all bow our heads in prayer."

I can't remember Mr. Evans's prayer word-for-word. It's been more than twenty years. But I think I can still manage its essence:

"Gawd, Our Father. We beseech Thee. A brilliant young leader has been shot. He is a man we love. He is a man

48

we trust. He is our president. Our Father, we beseech
Thee now to rest Your gentle hand upon this man and to
spare him, O Gawd. Spare him, so that he can continue to
lead us, to guide us, to keep us safe from our enemies,
to show us how to make our country even greater, to bring
justice to all our people, to make for these students,
who soon will go out into the world alone, a safe and
shining place to live and work and grow fruitful. Spare
John Kennedy, O Gawd. Spare our beloved president.
Amen."

We raised our heads. No one spoke. Some of the girls cried.

"Maybe it's not true," somebody finally said.

"It's true," said someone else, "or Mr. Evans wouldn't have stopped classes for it."

All doubt then faded. It *was* true.

We waited. I don't know how long we waited. Maybe it was seconds. Maybe it was minutes. Finally, the voice came back again.

"Students and faculty of Newnan High School," Mr. Evans began, "President John Fitzgerald Kennedy is dead."

The class idiot was Harley Doakes, whose father hated Kennedy because he had wanted to desegregate the schools. When Mr. Evans announced that the president was dead, Harley Doakes cheered. Somebody in the back of the room threw a book at him and called him a stupid son of a bitch.

* * *

Nothing was the same after that. Ever again. I trace my world going completely bananas back to that single moment

49

when the shots first cracked in Dallas.

What, if anything, has made any sense since? John Kennedy was dead and we were left with Lyndon Johnson, who was low enough to pick up a dog by its ears. He proceeds to get us involved up to *our* ears in Vietnam, and when he finally decides he's had enough, here comes Nixon again. Why wouldn't this man just go away?

I had all sorts of trouble trying to decide who I wanted to be president in 1972. Picking between Richard Nixon and George McGovern was like picking between sores in your mouth or a bad case of hemorrhoids. I wanted Nixon out, but I didn't want McGovern in.

McGovern was the hippie candidate. I had been raised a patriot. I reluctantly voted for Nixon. I admit he did a few things. He opened China, although I'm still not sure what good it did. If you've seen one Chinese urn, you've seen them all; I still don't know how to use chopsticks; and I never did like sweet and sour pork.

It was under Nixon that Vietnam finally came to a merciful end, of course, and there was that marvelous, moving moment when the POW's came home, but it was impossible for me to put heroic garb on Richard Nixon. There always was the nagging feeling each time I saw him or listened to him that he was somehow putting a Bobby Entrekin shuck on me.

Watergate was all I needed. There I had been a decade earlier — a high school senior with a crew cut and even clearer-cut ideals and values. Then the president is shot, and next comes Vietnam, and then somebody shoots Robert Kennedy, and Martin Luther King is gunned down, and another assassin puts George Wallace in a wheelchair for life. And on top of that, we find out the current president is, indeed, a crook (not to mention a liar with a filthy mouth) and he's run out of office practically on a rail.

I no longer had any idea what to believe or whom to trust. I was nearing thirty, and practically every sacred cow I had known had been butchered in one way or another.

Nothing was the same anymore. I had seen students burning campus buildings and students being gunned down on campuses by National Guardsmen.

I had been divorced once by then and was working on a second. Half the country was smoking dope. Gasoline was four times what it had cost before. Men were growing their hair over their ears and wearing double-knit trousers.

And they weren't singing the old songs anymore, either. In fact, it was soon after the death of John Kennedy that the music headed somewhere I didn't want to go.

If Elvis was a break between me and my parents and my roots, then it was The Beatles who forced me back toward them.

5 Where Rock 'n' Roll Went Wrong

AS MOST MUSIC historians know, soon after Elvis became the undisputed King, Colonel Tom Parker hid him out for nearly the next two decades. The only time we were able to see him was at a rare concert or in one of those idiotic movies he began making, such as *Viva Las Vegas,* which featured Elvis singing and mouthing ridiculous dialogue while several dozen scantily-clad starlets cooed and wiggled. Today, Elvis movies normally are shown very late at night after the adults have gone to bed, so they won't be embarrassed in front of their children.

However, the rock 'n' roll storm that Elvis started did not subside after he took leave of the public. As a matter of fact, the music flourished and reached new heights, and when it got its own television show, our parents' battle to save us from what some had considered a heathen sound was over. They had lost.

Dick Clark was apparently a very mature nine-year-old when he first appeared on "American Bandstand," because

52

that has been nearly thirty years ago and he still doesn't look like he has darkened the doors to forty.

Bandstand. I wouldn't miss it for free Scrambler rides and cotton candy at the county fair. The music they were playing was *our* music, and the dances they were dancing were *our* dances. It was live on television, and Philadelphia, from whence Bandstand came, was the new center of our universe. (Previously, it had been Atlanta, where our parents occasionally took us to see the building where they kept all the things you could order from the Sears Roebuck catalog, and to wrestling matches and gospel singings.)

Danny Thompson and I always watched Bandstand together in the afternoons. Danny was not nearly the geographical wizard I was (I had been born seventy-five miles from Moreland in Ft. Benning, Georgia, and had traveled as far away as Arkansas as the quintessential Army brat before my parents had divorced) so anything that had to do with where some place was, Danny asked me.

"Where is Philadelphia, anyway?" he queried one afternoon as we watched the kids on Bandstand do the Hop to Danny and the Juniors's "At the Hop."

"Pennsylvania," I told him.

"How far is that?"

"Thousands of miles."

"Wish I could go."

"To see Bandstand?"

"See it up close."

"Wish we lived in Philadelphia."

"We'd go on Bandstand every day, wouldn't we?"

Besides the music, Danny and I enjoyed watching Bandstand in order to select objects of lust from the group of Philadelphia girls who were regulars. I picked out a blonde

53

with large breasts. Her name was Annette something-or-other. Danny picked out a raven-haired beauty named Shirley, who chewed gum; we could never tell exactly how she voted when she rated a record because in the first place she talked funny, being from Philadelphia, and secondly it's difficult to discern what someone is saying when they're saying it through three sticks of Juicy Fruit gum.

We spent hours discussing whether or not, at their advanced ages of probably sixteen, they were engaging in any sort of sexual activity off camera.

"Wonder if Annette and Shirley do it?"

"I bet Annette does."

"Why?"

"She's got blonde hair. Blondes do it more than other girls."

"How do you know that?"

"My cousin told me. He said you see a girl who's blonde, and she'll do it."

"I'd like to do it with Annette."

"I'd like to do it with Shirley."

"Shirley's got black hair."

"I'd still like to do it with her."

"I'd give a hundred dollars to do it with Annette."

"I'd give two hundred to do it with Shirley."

"You don't have two hundred dollars."

"I could get it."

"How?"

"Sell my bicycle."

"You'd sell your bicycle to do it with Shirley?"

"You wouldn't sell yours to do it with Annette?"

"Maybe I would."

Of course, I would have. The desire to do it strikes young

in boys, and the delicious idea of doing it with a Bandstand regular was my first real sexual fantasy (which must be accepted as proof of our parents' fears that interest in rock 'n' roll did, indeed, prompt the sexual juices to flow).

* * *

The music was good back then. There were The Drifters, and The Penguins, and Paul and Paula, and Barbara Lewis, and Mary Wells, and Clyde McPhatter; and Sam Cook sang about the men workin' on the "chain ga-e-yang." We had Bobby Helms doing "Special Angel," and there was Jerry Butler talking about his days getting shorter and his nights getting longer. There were great songs like "A Little Bit of Soap" and "Duke of Earl" and Ernie Kado singing about his mother-in-law.

We danced and held each other close and took two steps forward and one back to "In the Still of the Night," and later we shagged to beach music — The Tams, The Showmen — and we twisted with Chubby Checker and did the Monkey with Major Lance. We had the soul sounds of James Brown — "Mr. Dynamite, Mr. Please Please Me Himself, the Hardest Workin' Man in Show Business" — and Jackie Wilson sang "Lonely Teardrops," and Marvin Gaye did "Stubborn Kind of Fellow," and Maurice Williams and the Zodiacs did "Stay." And I don't want to leave out Fats (Antoine) Domino and Chuck Berry and Joe Tex and Bobby Blue Bland and Soloman Burke and Jimmy Reed moaning over radio station WLAC, Gallatin, Tennessee, brought to you by John R., the Jivin' Hoss Man, and Ernie's Record Mart and White Rose Petroleum Jelly, with "a thousand-and-one different uses, and you know what that one is for, girl."

There were a thousand singers for a thousand songs. It was truly an enchanted time. But then ever-so-slowly yet ever-so-suddenly, it changed. It seemed that one day Buddy Holly died, and the next day The Beatles were in Shea Stadium.

I'm not certain what it was that caused me to reject The Beatles from the start, but I suspect that even then I saw them as a portent of ill changes that soon would arise — not only in music, but in practically everything else I held dear.

The Beatles got off to a bad start with me because the first thing I heard them sing in 1964 was "I Wanna Hold Your Hand," and it was basically impossible to do any of the dances I knew — the Shag, the Mashed Potato, the Monkey, the Pony, the Gator, the Fish, the Hitchhike, the Twist, or the Virginia Reel— to that first song. About all you could do to "I Wanna Hold Your Hand" was jump and stomp and scream, which, of course, is what every female teeny-bopper at the time was doing whenever The Beatles struck guitar and drum and opened their mouths.

Also, patriot that I was, I stood four-square against the importation of foreign music, just as I have since stood steadfastly against the importation of Japanese cars and Yugoslavian placekickers. The only materials we really need to import from foreign countries, in my way of thinking, are porno movies. It doesn't matter that you can't understand what anybody is saying in those movies anyway, and I like the imagination of, say, the French when it comes to doing interesting things while naked.

But the British? I still have problems with them, especially with the current royal family. I'm sick and tired of Lady Di getting pregnant, I don't care if Prince Andrew is dating Marilyn Chambers, and every time the Queen comes to the U.S., she is always getting offended by something a well-meaning colonist has done to her. I wish she would stay in Buckingham Palace and give the Cisco Kid his hat back.

Even then, I didn't like the way The Beatles looked. I thought their hair was too long, I didn't like those silly-looking suits with the skinny ties they wore, and Ringo reminded me of the ugliest boy in my school, Grady "The Beak" Calhoun, whose nose was so big that when he tried to look sideways he couldn't see out of but one eye. Grady was a terrible hitter on the baseball team because his nose blocked half of his vision.

Soon after The Beatles arrived in the U.S., I started college. At the fraternity house, we were able to hold on to our music for a time. The jukebox was filled with the old songs, and when we hired a band, we had black bands whose music you could dance to and spill beer out of your Humdinger milkshake cup on your date. The Four Tops and The Temptations, The Isley Brothers and Doug Clark and the Hot Nuts, and Percy Sledge (which always sounded to me like something that might clog your drain) were still in demand at college campuses — at least all over the South. A few white bands were still in vogue as well, the most notable of which was The Swinging Medallions. They sang "Double Shot of My Baby's Love," and even now when I hear that song, it makes me want to go stand outside in the hot sun with a milkshake cup full of beer in one hand and a slightly-drenched nineteen-year-old coed in the other.

But the music, our music, didn't last. At least, it didn't remain dominant. Elvis's music was switched to country stations, and every wormy-looking kid with a guitar in England turned up in the United States, and rock 'n' roll meant something entirely different to us all of a sudden.

57

I didn't like the new sounds or the new people who were making them. I found The Rolling Stones disgusting and The Dave Clark Five about a handful short.

Suddenly came the dissent associated with the Vietnam escalation, and with that came hippies and flower children. And one day I found myself (just as my own parents had done when Elvis peaked) condemning modern music as the hedonistic, un-American, ill-tempered, God-awful, indecent warblings of scrungy, tatooed, long-haired, uncouth, drugged-out, so-called musicians.

I didn't know Jimi Hendrix was alive until he overdosed and died, and I thought Janis Joplin was Missouri's entry in the Miss America pageant.

All the new groups had such odd names. There was Bread, and Cream, for instance. And there was Jefferson Airplane and Iron Butterfly and Grand Funk Railroad and a group named Traffic. I wondered why so many groups were named after various modes of transportation. I theorized that it was because those performers had all been deprived of electric trains as children.

I expected the members of musical groups to wear the same clothing when they performed — like white suits with white tails — and to do little steps together like "The Temptation Walk."

These new groups, however, apparently wore whatever they found in the dirty clothes hamper each morning before a performance. T-shirts and filthy jeans seemed to be the most popular garb. Some, of course, performed without shirts. I found this to be particularly disturbing, since I have no use whatsoever for any music made by a person who looks as if he has just come in the house from mowing the grass on an August afternoon and his wife won't let him sit down on the good furniture because he'll sweat all over it and probably cause mildew.

I didn't like drug songs and anti-war songs, and I didn't like songs that were often downright explicit. Even The Beatles just wanted to hold somebody's hand. The new groups, however, wanted to take off all their clothes, get in the bed, smoke a bunch of dope, and do all sorts of French things that have no business being watched, discussed, or sung about outside a porno flick on the sleazy side of town.

The only piece of raw rock 'n' roll we ever knew about before The Beatles came along was a song by The Kingsmen called "Louie, Louie," and we really weren't certain that what they were saying about "Louie, Louie" wasn't just a rumor.

It was basically impossible to understand the words, except the part which went, "Louie, Lou-eye, Ohhhhh, baby, we gotta go." After that, it sounded like, "Evahni ettin, Ah fackon nin."

The smart money had it, however, that if you slowed the record down from 45 RPM to 33 RPM, you could make out some of the words and that the song was really about doing something quite filthy. Naturally, we all rushed home to slow down the record. I still couldn't make out any of the words. It simply sounded like I was hearing the bass portion of "Evahni ettin, Ah fackon nin."

I made myself a vow never to spend money on any of this new music. But as naive as I was concerning what was taking place in my once placid, sensible world, I was bound to break my vow. I did so by attending an Elton John concert ... completely by mistake.

I was dating a girl who was several years younger than me. I was in my late twenties at the time, but she could still

59

remember where everybody sat in her high school algebra class.

"What do you want to do Friday night?" I vividly recall asking this young woman.

"Elton John is in town," she said.

"He's somebody you went to school with?" I asked, in all honesty.

"You've never heard of Elton John?" she said, an unmistakable tinge of amazement in her voice.

"Well, I've been working pretty hard and...."

"Elton John is a wonderful entertainer. You would love him."

She was a lovely child and had big blue eyes, so I managed to purchase excellent tickets for the Elton John concert — third row from the stage.

I had never been to a concert by anybody even remotely connected with modern rock music. As a matter of fact, the only concert I had been to in years was one that Jerry Lee Lewis gave. "The Killer" came out and did all his hits, and everybody drank beer and had a great time. I didn't see more than a dozen fights break out the entire night.

What I didn't know about attending an Elton John concert was that Elton didn't come on stage until his warm-up group had finished its act. I don't remember the name of the group that opened the show, but I do remember that they were louder than a train wreck.

When I was able to catch a word here and there in one of their songs, it sounded like the singer was screaming (as in pain) in an English accent. One man beat on a drum; another, who wasn't wearing a shirt, played guitar. They were very pale-looking individuals.

"What's the name of this group?" I tried to ask my date

60

over the commotion. I heard her say, "Stark Naked and the Car Thieves." I thought that was a strange name, even for an English rock group, so between numbers I asked her again. Turned out I had misunderstood her; their real name was "Clark Dead Boy and the Bereaved."

"So what was the name of that song?" I pursued.

" 'Kick Me Out of My Rut'," she answered. I was having trouble hearing, however; my eardrums had gone into my abdomen to get away from the noise. I thought she said, "Kick Me Out on My Butt."

After the next number, I asked her to name that tune, too.

"It's called 'I Can Smell Your Love on Your Breath'."

That's what she said, but what I heard was, "Your Breath Smells Like a Dog Died in Your Mouth," which sounded a great deal like "Kick Me Out on My Butt."

Finally, Elton John came out. He wore an Uncle Sam suit and large sunglasses.

"Is this man homosexual?" I asked my date.

"Bisexual," she answered.

That must come in handy when he has to go to the bathroom, I thought to myself. If there's a line in one, he can simply walk across to the other.

I had no idea what Elton John was singing about, but at least he didn't sing it as loudly as did Stark Naked and the Car Thieves.

As the concert wore on, I began to smell a strange aroma.

"I think somebody's jeans are on fire," I said. "Do you smell that?"

"It's marijuana," said my date. "Everybody has a hit when they come to an Elton John concert."

I looked around me. My fellow concert-goers, some of

61

whom weren't as old as my socks, were staring bleary-eyed at the stage. Down each row, handmade cigarettes were passed back and forth. Even when the cigarettes became very short, the people continued to drag on them.

Suddenly, down my row came one of the funny cigarettes. My date took it in hand, took a deep puff, held in the smoke, then passed it to me.

"No thanks," I said. "I think I'll go to the concession stand and get a beer."

"Go ahead," said my date. "It'll loosen you up."

This was my moment of decision. I had never tried marijuana before. I had never even seen any up close, but now here I sat holding some, listening to a bisexual Englishman wearing an Uncle Sam suit sing songs I didn't understand. I was completely lost in this maze and wanted to bolt from the concert hall and go immediately to where there was a jukebox, buy myself a longneck beer, and play a truck-driving son by Dave Dudley — something I could understand.

I looked at the marijuana cigarette again. Would I have an irresistible urge to rape and pillage if I took a drag?

It was very short. "You need a roach clip," said my date.

"There're bugs in this stuff?" I asked.

"When a joint is short like that, it's called a roach," she explained, pulling a bobby pin from her purse. "Hold it with this."

I took the pin in one hand and clipped it on the cigarette I was holding in the other.

"Take a good deep drag and hold it in," said my date.

"Suck it or send it down," said somebody at the end of my row.

I continued to look at the roach. The smoke got into my

WHERE ROCK 'N' ROLL WENT WRONG

eyes and they began to burn. Suddenly, to my horror, I noticed the fire at the end of the roach was missing. It had become dislodged from the clip and had rolled down between my legs. I quickly reached between my rear and the seat cushion to find it, lest I set the entire arena aflame.

"Hey, man," yelled the insistent one down the row, "where's that joint?"

"It's down here," I said, stooping over like a fool with my hand between my legs, searching for what was left of the marijuana.

"Groovy, man," he said. "I never thought of sticking it there."

Mercifully, Elton John finally completed his concert and I was free to leave.

"Well," said my date when we were in the car, "wasn't he great?"

"Save the fact that I burned a hole in the seat of my pants, burned my eyes from all the smoke, and lost partial hearing in both ears from attempting to listen to a nuclear explosion from the third row back, I suppose it wasn't all that bad."

"Good," she answered. "Let's go hear Reggae next. What do you think of Reggae?"

"I think he's the most overpaid outfielder in baseball," I answered.

That was our last date.

* * *

I honestly didn't think that the music and the people who made it could get worse than it was during the seventies, but again my naiveté was showing. What currently is regarded as "rock" is totally beyond me, especially when I'm switching around on my cable TV and come across one of those music video things.

In the first place, I don't understand what anybody is singing about. I heard a song on a video channel that was, appropriately enough, entitled "Radio."

The lyrics went like this:

"Radio. Radio. Radio.
Radio. Radio. Radio.
Radio. Radio. Radio."

An eleven-year-old child with a stuttering problem, I'm convinced, wrote that song.

Secondly, I do not understand what these people are doing when they're singing their songs on videos. I see people dressed like chickens, people singing while standing on their heads, and people — perhaps I'm using that term too loosely — diving into swimming pools filled with green Jell-O while they're still singing those songs. Every video I've ever seen has reminded me of the nightmares I have after eating too much Mexican food. It's music to throw-up by, I suppose.

I thought the names of the groups and the names of the songs were strange in the seventies, but the eighties have brought total insanity to popular music.

There are groups now like ZZ Top, The Cars, The Dead Kennedys, the B-52's, Run D.M.C., Duke Jupiter, Blond Ambition, Wall of Voodoo, The Cramps, The Razors, The Swimming Pool Q's, Modern Mannequins, Future Reference, The Divorcees, The Pigs, The Fabulous Knobs, Outa Hand, Late Bronze Age, Go Van Go, Riff-Raff, St. Vitus Dance, Kodac Harrison and Contraband, Subterraneans,

64

Corn, and Wee-Wee Pole.

Wee-Wee Pole? Now, somebody had to think of that name, and my imagination runs in all sorts of directions considering what prompted such a title for an alleged musical group. What comes to my mind first is this scene: There are a few guys snorting airplane glue or something in the back of their van, and one of 'em says, "Hey, why don't we start a band?", sort of a modern-day version of Mickey Rooney's Andy Hardy saying to Judy Garland and the gang, "Hey, why don't we give a show?"

Two other guys think this is a terrific idea, despite the fact that none of them has any musical talent whatsoever, which is no longer important if you want to start a band. The first order of business is to figure out what to call yourselves.

Before they can decide on a name, one of the guys indicates he needs to go to the bathroom, which reminds the others they need to do the same. So the entire group goes outside the van and begins to wee-wee on the first thing they see, which happens to be a telephone pole. The rest is history.

I seem to notice a pattern in names for rock groups today. The names usually either have to do with some sort of animal (The Pigs), something that doesn't make any sense whatsoever (Run D.M.C.) or something totally distasteful or vulgar (The Dead Kennedys and The Cramps).

If this is such a hot item, I would like to get into the business of naming rock groups myself. I likely could make a lot of money doing it, perhaps even start some sort of service. You send me twenty bucks, and I'll come up with a name for your rock group that will embarrass your parents to the point that they'll wish they'd come along when birth control was more widely accepted.

65

For groups that wanted animal names, I'd have Hog Wild and the Pork Bellies, Rabid Raccoon, Dead Dog and the Bloated Five, and Squid.

For names of rock groups that didn't make any sense whatsoever, the selection would include Oshkosh Ice Cream, Polished Cement, Snarknavel, and MDC Gravel.

In the totally disgusting and vulgar category, you could select from Umbilical Dan and the Chords, Potato Poothead, Battery Acid, Rat Poison, Willie and the Warts, and The Dingleberry Five.

You don't think things could ever get that weird with modern music? Of course, they can. Of course, they will. We've already got Michael Jackson, who sings a lot higher than Mahalia and probably lost his other glove doing something strange with Brooke Shields. (I once opined in another forum that if they ever made a remake of *Gone With the Wind,* Michael Jackson would make a perfect Butterfly McQueen's "Prissy.")

And then there's Boy George and Culture Club, of course. I've seen more culture on buttermilk.

Recently I heard a great curse: "May the next skirt you chase be worn by Boy George." What I want to know is, Does he shave his legs and have a period?

I have a theory about where all these people who make today's rock music came from. Remember when you were in high school and there were always a bunch of kids who were really thin and wormy, back when "punk" meant somebody who had a lot of zits and hung around playing pinball machines and never got asked to parties and never had dates and never played sports?

Well, they all grew up to be rock stars. That's what happened to them. It's the revenge of the nerds.

66

As much as I despise today's rock music, I must admit that it is even more popular with today's youth than Elvis's music was with my generation. I base this statement on the fact that I could go fifteen minutes to eat or to take a bath or to walk to school or to ride a bus without listening to my music. Kids today can't do that, so they have given the term portable radio an entirely new meaning. I'm talking about, of course, the Sony Walkman and the Ghetto Blaster Age that we are presently living through.

The Sony Walkman, I can take. Some adults even use these machines (which mercifully include earphones so nobody else will be disturbed) to listen to educational tapes and soft music that will put them to sleep in airplanes. I cannot resist the urge, however, when I see somebody tuned out of the regular world and tuned in to a taped version to ask, "What's the score?"

But ghetto blasters — which generally are about the size of a five-hundred-watt radio station — are something else entirely. Young people should be allowed to listen to any sort of music they like, but I shouldn't have to listen to it with them.

When I hear indecipherable music played two decibels above the sound the 4:15 flight to Cleveland makes when it takes off, it makes me nervous, unable to concentrate. And it eventually makes me angry enough to take the ghetto blaster from which the noise is emanating and stomp on it, even if doing so might mean having to defend my life against the owner, who suddenly has been deprived of something to get down on the street and dance on his head to.

Young people play their ghetto blasters on city streets where people with jobs are trying to have nervous breakdowns in peace. They play them on various forms of public transportation. They play them in fast-food restaurants or any time there is somebody else around to offend and render deaf.

There are laws against cursing in public, against spitting in public, against wee-weeing on telephone poles in public, and there should be laws against playing ghetto blasters in public.

* * *

This calamitous change in music, that began in the late sixties and has continued to the point of today's strange lyrics and stranger people, left me with a choice: Either I could totally change my tastes and my way of thinking and follow this metamorphosis, or I could look elsewhere and hope to find musical solace for the soul in another area.

I was lucky, in retrospect, to have had that second choice. The rock 'n' roll I knew was gone; I had absolutely no taste for music sung by fat ladies with high voices in a language I didn't understand; I have never liked any music where any part of it was made by an oboe or flute; I didn't mind a little Big Band now and then, and I could enjoy Sinatra on occasion, but that was my parents' music. Were it not for yet another choice, I might easily have become a musical orphan.

The war in Vietnam and the war against it at home were raging, and Americans had to pick a side. There were doves and flower children on one side and hawks and the guys at the VFW on the other. One kind of music raged against the war, while another kind was saying, "Love it or leave it."

It was Merle Haggard who gave me my new musical

direction. They used to say of Merle Haggard that he did all the things Johnny Cash was supposed to have done, such as serve time in prison.

It really didn't matter. Merle sang it sweet and from the heart, not to mention through the nose. He sang, "When you're runnin' down my country, Hoss, you're walkin' on the fightin' side of me." And he sang, "We don't smoke marijuana in Muscogee," and what I heard, I was drawn to. Now, pop open a longneck and let me tell you the rest of the story ... the best of the story.

They Call It Blue-Eyed Soul

I AM QUITE proud of the fact that I heard of Willie Nelson before most other Americans. This is sort of like being a style-setter and being one of the first people to know when white socks went out.

I'm not certain of the exact date when I first heard Willie sing and attached voice and song to name, but it was sometime during the late sixties after I had made the decision to abandon rock 'n' roll and place my musical interests elsewhere.

What eventually led me to country — before country was cool, if you'll allow me to steal a line from Barbara Mandrell — was, first, an Atlanta radio station changing its format. The station, WPLO-AM, had been a rock 'n' roll station during my youth, but when rock changed, so did WPLO. It went country.

It wasn't just that WPLO began playing country music, it was the way they played it that caught my ear. They avoided the cornball, which had been SOP for all country stations.

Remember the old country disc-jockeys back before country started washing its feet more than once a week?

"Hello there, friends and neighbors, this is your old Cuzzin Cholly, brangin' you some good ol' pickin' and fiddlin'. Yessiree, Bob, we gone have us a good time this here afternoon, and jist remember this here is all brought to you by Lon and Randy's Feed Store on the Pickett Road, yore hog pellet headquarters, and by them good folks over at the Piggly-Wiggly — my ol' Uncle Peahead calls that the Hoggly-Woggly — featuring bargains this week on neck bones, Cardui tablets, and septic tank aroma bars. Now, let's jist sit back and enjoy some good ol' country music. Here's a new'un by Nubbin Straker entitled 'I'm a Floatin' Corncob in the Slopjar of Love.'"

Such was offensive even to a ruralite like myself, who was quite familiar, indeed, with slopjars, the forerunner to the automatic garbage disposal.

I had occasionally drifted across WSM, clear-channel, Nashville, Tennessee, on Saturday nights and listened to the Grand Ole Opry, but even the commercials bothered me there. Somebody was always singing about Black Draught, which I seem to recall was a laxative, and about Goo-Goo Cluster candy bars.

What WPLO did was to put a disc-jockey on the air introducing country music who didn't sound like he just crawled out from under a slopjar, and nobody sang commercials about laxatives and candy, and I could understand the words to the music, and the singers sounded as though they didn't look like something that would crawl under the refrigerator when the lights went on in the kitchen.

Actually, my pilgrimage to country was a pretty short trip.

Despite my early affair with Elvis, nobody could grow up in a small rural town like Moreland, Georgia, in the 1950s and not have at least some appreciation for the way country music sounds when a jukebox is blaring it out from the inside of a truckstop on a hot, thick, summer's night, when the neon is bright and the bugs are bad.

My favorite of the two truckstops in Moreland was Steve's, where the waitress paid off on the pinball machines at the rate of ten cents an extra game; where the cheeseburgers were thick and greasy; where if you were tall enough to reach the counter, you were old enough to drink beer; and where they had an all-country jukebox that played twenty-four hours a day for what must have been fifteen years.

Once I learned in which directions the magnet pulled, I could easily turn fifty cents into a dollar-and-a-half at the pinball machines, and I spent many hours of my youth at that practice alongside the jukebox that was full of coins and country.

There was Hank Williams, still barely cold in his grave, and Faron Young, Little Jimmy Dickens, Eddy Arnold, Hawkshaw Hawkins, Cowboy Copas, Patsy Cline, Loretta Lynn, Hank Locklin, Roy Acuff, Ernest Tubb, Miss Kitty Wells, Gentleman Jim Reeves, the Wilburn Brothers, Lefty Frizell, Lonzo and Oscar, and Webb Pierce singing, among other great hits, "In the Jailhouse Now" and "There Stands the Glass."

In the late sixties, another generation of country stars began to blossom. Johnny Cash put on his black outfit and sang "Ring of Fire," and people talked about the time he had spent in prison, which apparently gave him credentials to wail about life's miseries.

Misery. That's what a lot of early country music was really

all about.

At the same time, former rockers like Conway Twitty and Jerry Lee Lewis were joining the fold, and they brought fans with them. Finally there was music that people like me, who thought Led Zeppelin had something to do with the octane level of gasoline, could listen to without getting a splitting headache.

Back in those days, Willie Nelson was just another short-haired Nashville songwriter. But once I heard him do a song called "Bloody Mary Morning" — she left last night and this is morning, and I might as well start drinking early so I can hurry up and pass out and forget her — I was hooked. He almost *talked* that song in a clear and piercing, if not somewhat nasal, tone. I hummed it for days.

Later, I heard him do "I Gotta Get Drunk and I Sure Do Hate It" and his own "Crazy" and "Ain't It Funny How Time Slips Away," and I became a devotee. I told other people about him, but they sort of looked at me sideways, the way a dog does when he's trying to figure out what on earth you're talking about. Pretty soon I got used to that look.

Despite the growing popularity of country music, there were still those holdouts who felt that all country wore a straw hat with the price tag hanging off (sorry, Miss Minnie). I picked up a date one evening, and when I started my car, the radio began playing George Jones doing the classic "Ol' King Kong Was Just a Little Monkey Compared to My Love for You."

My date immediately reached for the selector buttons on my radio and punched until she found some whiny Simon and Garfunkel song.

"What are you doing?" I asked in genuine horror.

"Somebody put your radio on a country station," said my

73

date, in the same voice she would have used to tell me a large dog had committed a horrid indiscretion in the front seat while I was out of my car.

This was not the same young woman who later dragged me to the Elton John concert, but they probably were second cousins now that I think back on it.

"*I* put my car radio on a country station," I said proudly.

The girl made a horrible face. Maybe a dog did commit an indiscretion on the front seat while I was out of my car. But no, it was worse. My date was turning up her nose at country music.

"You actually listen to that crap?" she asked.

"Crap?" I said. "You're calling country music crap?"

"That's exactly what it is. Crap."

"And what is that you're listening to?"

"Simon and Garfunkel."

"Hippie music."

"No, it isn't."

"Yes, it is. That kind of music is exactly what's wrong with this country."

"Are you some kind of Bircher or religious nut?" she asked.

"No," I said, "but I like country music and I don't like anybody who doesn't, and I will thank you to keep your communist, unpatriotic, ungracious fingers off my radio."

The girl asked to be put off at the next bus stop, which I was more than happy to do. I left her standing there, and as I drove off, I punched my country station back on and disappeared down the street — alone for the evening, but proud that I would not allow even the stirrings of lustful passion to come between me and George Jones.

This probably is how the Good Ol' Boy fraternity — a

74

fairly recently identified sociological group — got its start. Smart-aleck women, hippies, and other non-desirables began to make fun of us for enjoying country music, and we sort of banded together in retaliation. The offshoot was that we also went in directions opposite to those who scoffed at us, such as preferring cold beer in longneck bottles to white wine, pickup trucks to Volvos, and, in many instances, our dogs to women who would dare move our radio dials off a country music station.

Before long, country music was appealing to individuals who previously thought they were incapable of enjoying it. This phenomenon was called "crossover," which meant that even yankees had begun listening to country music without remarking about how corny it sounded. The first time I saw this conversion was in Chicago, where I was once held prisoner for three winters.

Powerful Chicago radio station WMAQ had recently changed its format to country and was running away with the ratings. The station even went as far as to sponsor a country concert at the Ivanhoe Theatre on the fashionable, trendy, north side. Billy "Crash" Craddock and Don Williams were the entertainers.

There wasn't an empty seat in the house, which was the first thing that surprised me. I didn't think that more than a handful of Chicagoans had ever heard of either artist. Crash Craddock came out in a red outfit with sparkling rhinestones, and instantly I thought I was back home in the National Guard Armory with Ernest Tubb on stage and every country girl within six counties down in front of the stage taking Ernest's picture while he sang, "It's a long ways from Nashville to Berlin, Honey, so keep them cards and letters comin' in."

Crash did all his big numbers, including the moving ballad "If I Could Write a Song," while midwestern ladies who had the night off from the bowling leagues snapped pictures of him and his funky Santa suit.

It was Don Williams, however, singing soft and low, who stole the show. He came out wearing a floppy hat — the kind Gabby Hayes used to wear — and proceeded to sing non-stop for two hours. When he was done, three thousand frostbitten yankees stood as one and cheered his marvelous, mellow performance.

He had done "Amanda," of course, and "You're My Best Friend" and "She Never Knew Me." And during his encore, I felt I was at some sort of evangelical celebration where the entire audience suddenly had seen the light and had come forward en masse for the altar call.

The entire evening had, in fact, been a wonderful religious experience, and I do not make a spiritual allusion here without basis.

Remember Tom T. Hall's "I Remember the Year Clayton Delaney Died"? Clayton Delaney, so the song went, had been an extraordinary guitar-picker (that's different from "guitarist"), and he also drank a bit and was a rounder. But as he lay dying, the story went on, Clayton Delaney got religion. Tom T. finished the ballad with the suggestion that Clayton's deathbed conversion, and the fact that he could flat pick, probably led him to his just reward. Sang Tom T. in the last verse:

> *"I know there's a lot of good preachers,*
> *Who know a lot more than I do.*
> *But it could be the Good Lord*
> *Likes a little pickin', too."*

76

* * *

The pure state of country music — once called "blue-eyed soul" — was bound to go the route of all else once good and simple, of course. I don't know who or what is to blame for the fact that country has forsaken its roots. Today flutists are playing background (and probably oboists, too, although I don't think I would recognize the sound of an oboe if I heard it), country stars are making movies, New York has its own country music night club and radio station, the rhinestones have been replaced by tight jeans and occasionally even tuxedos, nobody remembers Faron Young or Webb Pierce anymore, and half of what you hear that's supposed to be country today isn't country at all, but rather some sort of unholy mix better left for Wee-Wee Pole and the other musical fruits.

We have to start somewhere in tracing what caused country to go cosmopolitan, however, so I think we should start with Dolly Parton's breasts.

It's not Dolly Parton's fault that she has big breasts, and I dare say she still would be a rare talent without her chesty appearance. However, when Dolly Parton became a big country star, people started noticing her breasts more than her singing. Suddenly everybody else wanted to get into the act, and sex subsequently found its way on country stations where once Miss Kitty Wells, in ankle-length skirt and cowgirl boots, had trod.

Pretty soon the Mandrell sisters were wiggling a lot, and the girls on "Hee Haw" were half-naked for each performance, and Conway Twitty was singing, "Pardner, there's a tiger in those tight-fittin' jeans."

77

Has anyone noticed the sexual overtones that have found their way into modern country music? Conway ought to have his mouth washed out. He sang another song about "Even with your hair up in curlers, I'd still love to lay you down." And there was the one where he sang about the girl "who had never been this far before, bum-bum-bum," and he even had the audacity to remake a Pointer Sisters hit, where he suggests, "You want a lover who will spend some time; not come and go with a heated rush."

Country singers today think nothing of crooning about "the first time we went all the way," and "When we were down to nothing, nothing sure looked good on you," and "If I don't feel like a man, feel again." All of this likely would leave an old pioneer purist like Roy Acuff with his yo-yo in a knot.

I also blame Willie Nelson for a lot of this country-gone-chic. I could overlook the beard and the headband and the ponytails, but then he went one step over the line.

I was at a Willie concert, all ready to cry in my beer and stomp my feet. Then I noticed that the crowd was changing a bit. There was the cowboy-hatted contingent and the GOB's, but there were also people apparently leftover from that Elton John concert, and those weren't Marlboros they were smoking.

Willie put on his usual grand show. He opened, as always, with "Whiskey River," and then he did a medley of his older material. He knocked us over with "The Red-Headed Stranger," which has an ending line that always brings a cheer from the male contingent in the audience: "You can't hang a man for killing a woman who was trying to steal his horse."

It was somewhere in "The Red-Headed Stranger (From

Blue Rock, Montana)," as a matter of fact, that I noticed something strange about Willie Nelson.

He was wearing an earring. Or, at least, he appeared to be wearing an earring. I asked a companion sitting next to me to verify my observation.

"Damn if he ain't," was his reply.

It took me a week or so to figure out how I felt about such a thing. To begin with, I naturally had some doubts about a man wearing an earring, the same sort of doubts I would have had about a man wearing undershorts with pictures of flowers on them. I don't even think Elton John wore an earring, and I'm certain you could have threatened to bash Ernest Tubb's guitar and he still would have refused to wear an earring.

I doubt seriously if there's anything in the Bible that warns against men wearing earrings, but there should be. "Woe be unto ye if ye stick an earring in thy ear and aren't named Rachel or Ruby Ann," is what it should say.

I was pleased at first that country music had become so universally accepted, but did that mean country music eventually was going to lose all its purity? The way Willie Nelson sang, I supposed I could overlook the earring, too, but where would all this eventually lead?

Crossover not only meant their coming to us, I determined, but it also could mean our going over to them. Would we have bisexual country stars and country stars who dressed as bats and stuck out their tongues at the audience? Would country music no longer embrace its classic subjects — cheatin' and fightin' and truckin' and drinkin' and cryin' — but begin to embrace drugs and anarchy? Would the time come when I could no longer differentiate between country music and rock music, because all music would have

79

blended into a form without identity?

These were troubling thoughts. If country music lost its identity, if it were swallowed up into a giant, black hole where electronic gadgets screamed and screeched, where drums pounded out ancient rhythms, who would be left to sing for those of us who fed it during its hungry years?

Willie Nelson wearing an earring. He had told us in "I'd Have to Be Crazy" that he had grown a beard "just to see what the rednecks would do," but did he have to give us this rigid a test?

I never quite forgave Willie Nelson for the earring, but I continued to listen to his music, giving him the benefit of the doubt. I figured he was on the road so much that he didn't get a balanced diet, which caused him to be constipated a lot, which is a direct cause of strange behavior. A person who is constipated all the time suffers great fits of anxiety that go along with it, and maybe Willie had been so anxious that it had affected his ability to think clearly. So one day he said to himself, "I think I'll buy an earring and stick it in my ear, and maybe that'll take my mind off being constipated."

How I wish Willie had consulted me before he did that. A few swigs of Milk of Magnesia probably would have had the same effect and wouldn't have been nearly as unsettling to his fans.

* * *

Here's what I wish would happen to country music: I wish they would give it back to the loyalists and the traditionalists.

I wish somebody would start a new brand of music called "Neo-Country" or "Randy Rural," and anybody who

80

wanted to sing with flutes and oboes and loud guitars, and sing lyrics you would be embarrassed for your mother to hear, could go off and listen to that. The rest of us, including Willie and his pal Waylon, could go on back to Luckenbach, Texas, and get back to the basics of country music.

I want the kind of country music George Jones sings. George sings like a steel guitar sounds. I want to hear more of George singing "If drinkin' don't kill me, then her memory will."

I want Willie to take out the earring and sing more songs like "Faded Love," that he did with Ray Price, and "Railroad Lady," that he did in memory of Lefty Frizell. In recent times, Willie has sung with Spaniard Julio Iglesias, and he's making an album with Frank Sinatra. Where will it end — Willie and Pavarotti singing opera together?

I want more Moe Bandy rodeo songs. I want more pure sounds like Larry Gatlin, more lyrical quality like Tom T. Hall brings to his music. I want Gene Watson and Rex Allen, Jr., and a few Chet Atkins instrumentals and less Eddie Rabbitt. Said my boyhood friend and idol, Weyman C. Wannamaker, Jr., a great American, who is also a country music fan, "If that mess Eddie Rabbitt sings is country, my dog's a P-H-damn-D."

I want Kenny Rogers to take a few months off and never sing another song like "Coward of the County." I want George Strait to make more songs like "Amarillo by Morning," with those mournful fiddles in the background. I never want to hear John Anderson sing "Swingin" again.

I don't want Alabama to do anymore truck-driving songs like "18-Wheeler." Dave Dudley and Red Sovine should do truck-driving songs; Alabama should do "Old Flame" and "She's a Lady, Down on Love."

I want more Joe Stampley and more country songs like "You're a Hard Dog to Keep Under the Porch" and "Don't Come Home a-Drinkin' with Lovin' on Your Mind" and less like "If I Said You Had a Beautiful Body, Would You Hold It Against Me?"

I want country songs with twin-fiddle intros, and I want Charley Pride to do what he does best — sing the old songs Hank used to sing — and I want Hank, Jr., to forget the hard country and try singing the sweet songs that make you want to cry and call your ex-wife and ask for forgiveness, like Don Williams sings.

I want Conway Twitty to clean up his act, but I don't want Merle Haggard to change a thing.

Country music is too much fun to allow it to be spoiled. No other sort of music offers such classic lines:

— "If fingerprints showed up on skin, wonder whose I'd find on you?"

— "My wife just ran off with my best friend, and I miss him."

— "You're the reason our children are ugly."

— "If you're gonna cheat on me, don't cheat in our home town."

— "I've got the all-overs for you all over me."

— "It's not love, but it's not bad."

— And the immortal: "I gave her a ring and she gave me a finger."

I also believe that all country music should fall under one of the following categories:

— CHEATIN' SONGS: She ran off.

— LOVIN' AND FORGIVIN' SONGS: She came back.

— HURTIN' SONGS: The hussy ran off again.

— DRINKIN' SONGS: Nobody here to cook me anything

to eat, so I might as well get drunk.
— TRUCKIN' SONGS: She run off on a train. I think I'll
derail that sucker.
— PRISON SONGS: They take derailing trains serious in
Mississippi.
— RODEO SONGS: Soon as she got out of the hospital after
the train wreck, she took up with a bullrider.
— NEVER-GIVE-UP-HOPE SONGS: I wonder if her sister
still lives in Tupelo.

* * *

I've taken a lot of abuse in my lifetime for being a country
music fan, but it's all been worth it. Quite frankly, country
music has helped me through many tough times. Whatever
the problem, there's always meaning in country music,
something to lean on.

Want to know what's really important in life? Country
music has the answer to that in Tom T. Hall's "Old Dogs,
Children, and Watermelon Wine":

"Old dogs care about you,
Even when you make mistakes.
And God bless little children,
While they're still too young to hate.
I tried it all when I was young,
And in my natural prime.
Now, it's old dogs and children,
And watermelon wine."

Freedom. There are times I have paid dearly to get it or to
regain it. Perhaps I should have listened to Kris Kristoffer-

son:

*"Freedom's just another word
For nothin' left to lose...."*

There is something about country music that should appeal to every writer, to everyone who has something in his heart and wants others to feel what he feels.

I've written lots of country songs, myself. Unfortunately, nobody has ever bothered to record one, but that still doesn't stop me from having a few beers occasionally and knocking out a few country lyrics — which is the way most country songs come to be written. People who write rock songs, on the other hand, apparently do so while being stoned (in the Biblical sense).

I've written some very poignant country songs, as a matter of fact. After a six-pack one night, I came up with this one:

*"Singles bars ain't no place,
Ain't no place for a lady.
It's dark, talk is cheap,
And the men are all shady.
But where does she go,
And is it so wrong,
When a lady's been single too long?"*

Impressed? That's nothing. I also wrote:

*"You say she gave you her number, friend
Well ain't that just fine.
I know it's Heartbreak six, fourteen-ten,*

84

'Cause that number used to be mine."

I even wrote a train song once, and it went something like this:

> *"Sweet, sweet Jesus,*
> *I never gave you thanks*
> *That once as a youth,*
> *Through the middle of Georgia,*
> *I rode the Nancy Hanks."*

Sometimes when the lyrics won't come, when the beer won't go down easy, I write titles instead. I have some wonderful new titles just waiting for words.

How about, "I'd Marry Your Dog Just to Be a Part of Your Family"?

Or, "Who's Gonna Cut My Toenails After You're Gone?"

I like this one, too: "You Threw Up On the Carpet of My Love;" or, "You'll Never Get Away From Me Darling, Because Even When You're Taking a Shower with Somebody Else, I'll Be the Soap on Your Rag."

The words to that one will probably go something like this:

> *"I know I whine a lot*
> *And occasionally I nag,*
> *But you'll never get away from me, darling,*
> *'Cause even when you're taking a shower*
> *With somebody else,*
> *I'll be the soap on your rag."*

I admit it needs a little work, but at least you get the idea.

Perhaps the real point here is that when Elvis and rock 'n' roll came along and caught me as a boy, I followed them off despite my parents' rages against them. But when they led too far, country music called me back, and I forevermore will be grateful. Without it, who knows? I might have wound up one day with hair down to my shoulders, sandals on my feet, a ghetto blaster over my shoulder, and smelling like The Goat Man.

The Goat Man? He may have been the original hippie.

# A Hairy Ode To The Goat Man

TAKE IT ALL down to the lowest common denominator, shake off all the dust and heave out all the bull, and most of the problems we had with each other in the late sixties and early seventies really were about hair.

Think about it. Let's suppose that student protesters who were burning buildings and marching and demonstrating against the war in Vietnam had shown up at the rallies wearing khaki pants, nice button-down, blue Oxford-cloth shirts, Weejuns, and short hair. I contend we wouldn't have had near the commotion that we did.

Older people would have looked at them and instead of saying, "You godless, bed-wetting, pinko, Commie, nasty, long-haired hippies," they might have said, "Gee, those youngsters certainly are vocal against the war, but isn't it wonderful to see boys and girls that age taking an active interest in government."

I'm not certain why, but most rebellions, however small, usually start with somebody doing something funky with their hair. Remember that at the Boston Tea Party, American revolutionaries grew their hair long, put it up in ponytails, donned feathers, and went out and started a war. Almost two hundred years later, a bunch of actors started a rebellion on Broadway with a musical called *Hair*. Some things never change.

The history of my own hair is one of coming and going.

When I was a baby, so my mother says, I had blond curls. She cut them off and still has them in a box somewhere. She can keep them.

When I was old enough to have my first haircut, my father, the soldier, took me to a barber shop and had them cut all my hair off. I doubt that he asked the barber to sweep my chopped locks off the floor so he could keep them in a small box, because like most military men, my father had no use for hair whatsoever. I never would have attempted to grow Elvis ducktails, had I lived with my father at the time, for fear he would have called me "Louise" instead of the name they gave me.

After I got over the ducktails thing, I went back to a crew cut because that's what all the other boys wore. I allowed the crew cut to grow out before I started college, but I remained a relative skinhead through college and into my early adult years. I didn't want anybody to think I was having anything to do with the hippie and anti-war movements.

Actually, I never saw a live hippie until after I was out of college. Come to think of it, I didn't see any dead ones, either. The University of Georgia was not exactly a hotbed of activism when I was in school there between 1964 and 1968. We were too busy enjoying the school's recent upsurge in football success after a long Dark Age. The only drugs I knew about were those pills you took to stay up all night and study because you'd been drinking beer and partying all weekend, celebrating Georgia's victory over Auburn.

I distinctly remember the first hippie-in-the-flesh I ever saw. The year was 1968. I had just taken a job in Atlanta. One day I was driving along Peachtree Street and entered the 10th Street area, once known for a country music juke joint called Al's Corral. Often had I been to Al's, where the beer was cold and the music made you want to cry.

But by 1968, the 10th Street area had changed. It had become the Deep South's answer to Haight-Asbury.

Hippies were everywhere — tall hippies, short hippies, boy hippies, and girl hippiettes. Gaggles of hippies sat on the sidewalks; one played guitar, while the others sang along or sat quietly listening to the music or picking their feet.

I must admit that I have done, and still do, my own share of foot-picking, but I consider it an exercise that should take place only in private and only occasionally. A person who picks his feet more than twice a month probably has some serious mental disorder, possibly dating back to his youth when he went around barefooted in the front yard and suffered stubbed toes or came down with planter's warts from stepping on places where frogs went to the bathroom. (It is common knowledge that one thing that causes warts is frog pee-pee. You probably could look it up in a medical book somewhere.)

Foot-picking, I also admit, can be an enjoyable experience. When I pick my feet, maybe once every three or four months, I first dig under my toenails and remove any foreign matter such as sock lint. Then I rub my fingers between my toes, which also removes weird stuff that hides in there. Rubbing between your toes makes you tingly all over.

Next, I pick at any callouses on the bottom of my feet. Since I rarely go barefoot anymore, especially outdoors where I might step into some frog pee-pee, I don't have to worry about warts.

I conclude my foot-picking by washing my hands thoroughly.

As I sat at a traffic light on Peachtree Street in the 10th Street area that day back in 1968, I watched one hippie in particular who apparently thought nothing of picking his feet in front of five o'clock traffic on the busiest street in town.

He had taken off his sandals and parked them next to him on the curb. I never could have been a hippie, if for no other reason than because I refuse to wear sandals, the official shoe of hippiedom. Sandals look awful, especially if you wear long, dark socks with them.

As a boy, I had noticed tourists from up north who were driving through Moreland on their way to Florida and had stopped at Bohannon's Service Station for gasoline. Yankee men tourists inevitably wore Bermuda shorts and sandals and long, black socks they pulled up almost to their armpits. Occasionally, however, a yankee tourist would come through and go to the other extreme. He would roll his socks down all the way to his ankles, which made him and his sandals look even sillier. I vowed never to wear sandals, even if it meant walking through a frog latrine barefooted.

I continued to watch the hippie pick at his feet. He dug under a nail with concentration and resolve. Since he wore no socks at all, I knew it wasn't sock lint he was removing. Perhaps it was road tar or some sort of animal leavings. The man looked as if he'd been sleeping with goats.

After completing his nail work, the hippie turned his

90

attention to between his toes. I don't know what causes strange substances to get between your toes, especially if you're in an urban setting and far from the nearest chicken yard. But I do know from personal experience that if you don't wash your feet often and your feet sweat a lot, you will have a gooey material between your toes. This substance normally is referred to as toe jelly or toe cheese. Since hippies seldom washed their feet, I figured he had a blue-ribbon supply of toe jelly between his toes.

At any rate, the light finally changed, and I drove away convinced that besides the political differences between me and hippies, there was one other major difference: I don't pick my feet in public.

That was just one of the reasons I never considered becoming a hippie, of course. Another was that they reminded me too much of The Goat Man, who is another story.

* * *

Once or twice a year, when I was growing up, The Goat Man would come through Moreland and park his goats and the wagon they pulled in front of the Masonic Hall, where he would camp for a couple of days.

The Goat Man had a long beard and wore tattered clothing and a pair of high-top tennis shoes, which he probably slept in. When, and if, The Goat Man ever got around to picking his feet, he probably found all sorts of things between his toes — even small animals that had gone there to hibernate for the winter.

The Goat Man was a fairly nice person, if you could stand the smell. Herds of goats give out a distinctive aroma, reminiscent of chitterlings while they're being cooked. People who live with herds of goats and sleep in their tennis shoes in the back of wagons take on the smell of their goats, which mixes with their own noxious odor, thereby creating a blend that would shock the olfactory nerves of a buzzard.

The Goat Man always carried around chewing gum for the children who came to see him and his goats, and we normally could hold our breath just long enough to get a couple of sticks of Juicy Fruit from him before we had to run for fresh air.

The Goat Man told great stories, though.

"Been all the way to Alaska and back since I was here last," he would say. "Got so cold, I had to sleep between my goats to keep warm."

Somebody would ask how long it took him to get to Alaska and back.

"These old goats here," he would answer, pointing to his herd, "were just babies when I left. They were great-grand-parents by the time we got back."

The more I think about it, perhaps The Goat Man *was* the original hippie. He spurned the establishment life and indi-cated that he would rather share his being with goats than with other people.

I'm not certain if The Goat Man is still alive, or if he even lived long enough to see the hippie movement. I sort of hope he did, and I hope he took credit for starting it. A man who has spent his life huddling against the cold between goats needs to know he has left some sort of legacy, no matter how much it might smell.

* * *

There were certain beliefs, whether real or imagined, concerning hippies that were strongly held by those of us outside the movement.

There was the hair thing, of course. It was The Beatles who first hid their ears under their locks, but the hippies took it further and grew their hair over their shoulders and down even to their rears. And they grew long beards. That is, the male hippies grew long beards. Girl hippiettes, most of whom couldn't grow beards, allowed the hair under their arms and on their legs to grow.

In some cultures, men find female underarm hair to be quite desirable. Not so with American men — not even hippies, I would wager. That makes me somewhat suspect of one of those beliefs we had about hippies, that their "Make love, not war" ideas meant they were spending a lot of time having sex with one another.

I really doubt that now. Sleeping with goats is one thing, but making love to a hairy-legged girl with hairy underarms is an even more disgusting notion. I suspect that when we thought hippies were having all that sex, they probably weren't doing anything more intimate than picking one another's feet.

We firmly believed that hippies didn't wash their hair often and probably had cootie bugs roaming around on their scalps.

I'm not exactly certain what a cootie bug is, but there was a boy in my school whose head was allegedly infested with them. He was always scratching at his scalp, and he soon absorbed the nickname (or should I say nickmane?) of "Coot." The teacher finally called the health department and they came and got "Coot" and gave him some sort of treatment. He never scratched his head much after he was de-cootied, which was one of the first miracles of modern medical techniques I ever saw.

It was the fact that hippies wore their hair long and probably had cootie bugs that caused me to begin shampooing every day. Previously, I had not shampooed more than once or twice a week, because when I did my hair would become quite dry and stick up all over my head. A date once remarked that it looked like I was wearing a cocker spaniel on my head. I decided, however, that it would be easier to get another date than to get rid of cootie bugs.

It was the order of that day to make fun of hippies' long hair. The most popular game was to question the gender of a male hippie whose hair flowed down his back like Trigger's tail.

"See that?" somebody would ask, pointing to a nearby hippie.

"I see it, but I don't know what it is," would come the reply.

"Is it male or female?"

"Can't tell."

"It's wearing a man's clothes."

"But it's got hair like a girl."

"Maybe it's one of them she-men. They got those operations now, you know."

"Naw, it's just one of them nasty-headed hippies."

"Yeah, see it doin' that peace sign? All them hippies give that peace sign."

"Yeah, well give the son of a bitch half of it back."

The truth is, those of us in the straight world didn't like hippies and didn't trust them and wanted them to go away so our world could go back to being normal.

We wanted to win the war in Vietnam and bring the boys home victorious and have ticker tape parades for generals

94

and show the evil communistic world that you don't mess with the United States of by-God America. Hippies wanted peace, even a dishonorable one. The cowards.

Hippies smoked dope and took LSD and God knows what else. We wondered why they couldn't be satisfied with beer like the rest of us.

Hippies liked flowers. We liked football.

Hippies listened to musical groups with names like Led Zeppelin and Cream and Jefferson Airplane and Blind Faith and The Grateful Dead and The Moody Blues. We still liked Merle Haggard and "Okie From Muscogee."

"Leather boots are still in style if a man needs foot-wear.
Beads and Roman sandals won't be seen.
And football's still the roughest thing on the campus.
And the kids here still respect the college dean."

Hippies looked filthy. We smelled like Aqua-Velva men.

Hippies didn't work. We busted our tails for promotions.

Hippies wore sandals and patched jeans. We wore wing tips and three-piece suits.

Hippies joined communes. We joined the Rotary Club.

Hippies danced nude in the mud. We worked on our golf games.

There were, of course, many people in my age group who broke away and went off to become hippies. I knew of only one, however. He was Stinky Drake, who was from Moreland and was a couple of years older than me.

As I look back, I can see now that even as a child Stinky showed evidence that one day he might grow up to be a hippie. He never played baseball with the rest of us. He spent his time making belts and Indian moccasins from a kit

95

he had ordered from an ad in the *Grit* newspaper. He did other strange things, too, like the time we went on a Boy Scout trip and we caught a large number of catfish and tied them on a stringer. When nobody was looking, Stinky took the fish off the stringer and set them free.

"What if you were a fish?" Stinky asked his irate camp-mates. "Would you want to be stuck on a stringer, or to be free to go back to your family in the river?"

We realized there was no point in arguing with anybody who worried about fish being taken from their families, so we tied Stinky to a tree and went back to breaking up fish families for our evening meal. Stinky wouldn't eat that night because he said it would make him feel guilty eating some-body's father or mother.

It wasn't long afterwards that Stinky became the first vegetarian I ever met. At school they served him a special plate; nobody would eat with him and Stinky soon became known as "Bean Breath."

In high school, Stinky joined the Drama Club and wrote a poem for the school paper entitled "An Ode to Vegetables." I remember the closing lines:

> *"Just because I don't eat meat*
> *Doesn't mean that I'm not neat."*

I suppose we were cruel to Stinky, which caused him to rebel against the norm even more. After he graduated from high school, we heard he went off in the mountains some-where and ate a lot of roots and berries and lived on what he could earn selling the belts and Indian moccasins he still made.

Next, we heard that he had broken his parents' hearts by

growing his hair long and taking up dope-smoking and running off to Canada to avoid the draft. He also was living in in sin with a woman who didn't wear shoes or shave under her arms. He had met her at a rock concert.

I don't have any idea what ever happened to Stinky, but I suppose he's still out there in the hills somewhere, dressed like Cochise and munching on sunflower seeds.

* * *

It is odd — and beneficial, too — how time changes ideas and mends feelings. After the war in Vietnam ended, most of the hippies bathed themselves, cut their hair, quit wearing sandals, and quit picking their feet. Today most of them are stockbrokers or fertilizer salesmen.

But they left their mark, and again it was the hair. Do you know who wears their hair long today? Good ol' boys, that's who. You can see it coming out from under their International Harvester and Red Man caps. Know who wears their hair neat and short? Gays and those men you see in clothing ads in the Sunday *New York Times Magazine* (although that may be a redundancy).

As for my own hair, here's the rest of the shaggy story:

After the war, longer hair became the accepted fashion for men, and I followed suit. Sideburns even made a comeback. I had long hair and sideburns, and all of a sudden it wasn't possible to go to a regular barber shop anymore. Men had to go to stylists, and where they once had paid three bucks for a haircut, it was now costing them $12.50 and they had to make an appointment.

The first time I went to a hair stylist — it was around 1974 — I made an appointment with the renowned Mr. Phyllis.

97

"What on earth have you been shampooing with, my dear boy?" asked Mr. Phyllis.

"Soap," I said.

"Oh, God, no," Mr. Phyllis recoiled in horror. "Soap dries the hair and splits the ends."

I started to say my end had been split my entire life, but I decided it would not be wise to talk about such while I was alone in the room with Mr. Phyllis.

He immediately took charge of my hair. He shampooed it with an odd-smelling substance, put conditioner on it, and then "sculptured" it. Finally he put the blow dryer to me, and when it was over, I paid him the $12.50.

I felt a little cheated. At the barber shop, not only had I been charged a mere three bucks, but the barber usually told me a joke, too.

"Fellow had these two sows he wanted to get mated," went my barber's favorite joke. "He didn't have a boar, but he knew a fellow who did. So he called him up and asked if he could bring his two sows up to his farm and let that ol' boar have a go at 'em.

"The fellow said to bring 'em on up, so he put the two sows in the back of his pickup and drove 'em to his neighbor's farm.

"That ol' boar got real interested in his job and really did some work on the two sows. There was all sorts of gruntin' and oinkin' goin' on, 'cause when you got three thousand pounds of pork in the heat of passion, you got something wild.

"Anyway, when the ol' boar was finished, the man asked his neighbor how he would know if the job had took. His neighbor said to look out at his hogs the next morning, and if they were layin' up in the sunshine, everything was okay.

98

But if they were still wallowin' in the mud, he'd have to bring 'em back.

"Next morning, he looked out his window and his hogs were wallowin' in the mud, so he put 'em back in his truck and drove 'em back to see the boar again.

"Same thing happened. His neighbor's wife broke out in a sweat watchin' them hogs, and the dogs got to barkin' loud and they had to throw cold water on 'em.

"Next mornin', though, it was the same thing. Them two hogs was still wallowin' in the mud. Man took his hogs up there a third time. Next mornin', he couldn't bear to look out at his hog pen, so he said to his wife, 'Honey, look out there and tell me if my hogs are sittin' in the sunshine or wallowin' in the mud.'

"She looked out the window and said, 'Neither one.'

"The man said, 'Well, where are they?'

"The fellow's wife said, 'One of 'em's in the truck ridin' shotgun, and the other one's blowin' the horn.'"

Mr. Phyllis didn't know any jokes, or at least not any like that. He was always too busy talking about his cat or watering the plants in his salon to tell jokes.

After I had gone to the trouble of having my hair styled, I thought it would be wise to take care of what my $12.50 had bought me, so I vowed never to wash my hair with soap again and went out to buy some shampoo.

"Do you have any shampoo for men?" I asked a saleslady in the cosmetics department.

"I think you will like this," she answered, handing me a bottle of shampoo. "It has the faint aroma of apricot."

Apricot?

"If you don't care for apricot," the woman continued, "perhaps you would like something with an herbal essence."

What I really wanted, I said, was something that smelled like soap. I didn't want to go around with my head smelling like a fruit salad.

I also purchased an electric hair dryer, of course. Previously, I had allowed my hair to dry naturally. When I was in a hurry, I would simply shake my head back and forth like a dog does when he's wet. With longer hair, however, I was told that this was impossible, even though I knew I'd seen a collie dry itself off with just two or three good shakes.

After purchasing the hair dryer, I also had to buy hairspray. When I bought it, I said a silent prayer that my father wasn't somewhere looking down upon his only son buying gook that sprayed out of a can to keep my hair in its original, upright and locked position after it had been blown dry and styled each morning.

But it had been so much simpler for my father. He hadn't needed shampoo or hair dryers or hairspray, because nobody else used anything like that when he was a young man about town. Men were men in his day. He would have hit Mr. Phyllis square in the mouth if that dandy had tried to sculpt his hair.

The hair situation is even more confusing today. Mine is shorter than it was when I first allowed it to grow in the seventies, but it still covers my ears. I got rid of the sideburns, but now I've got a beard and a mustache. I'm not certain what my father would think of that.

"Ain't but two kinds of people who wear beards and mustaches," he likely would have said. "That's queers and movie stars, and I ain't seen none of your movies lately."

But if he's concerned about my hirsute appearance, I wonder what he thinks about punk rockers who have their hair styled to look like the back of a horned frog. And I

100

wonder what he thinks of people these days who dye their hair all sorts of colors, including orange and pink. My only hope is that heaven has mellowed him.

But what of me? I'm still here trying to deal with all this craziness. Hair and music have been a problem, but I have managed to cope with them after some degree of agony. But there have been so many other changes and dilemmas in the modern world. For instance, whose idea was it that men all of a sudden were supposed to be sensitive and enjoy fooling around with flowers and were even supposed to cry in front of women if they felt like it?

Each time I thought I knew all the answers to modern-day questions, somebody would up and change the questions.

And just when I thought there was nothing left to go haywire, I lost complete touch with the reality that was once men's clothing.

Excuse me for a moment, while I change into my leisure suit.

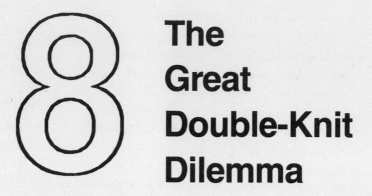

The Great Double-Knit Dilemma

WHEN WE'RE YOUNG, we naturally attempt to dress as our peers do, lest we be ostracized and laughed at. My wardrobe in college, for instance, consisted of the traditional khaki pants and button-down Gant shirts, a couple of V-neck sweaters, a London Fog raincoat, and a pair of Weejuns.

I also had a couple of pairs of socks, but I wore them only to funerals, weddings, or when I had to visit the dean. It was considered quite the fashion not to wear socks with Weejuns. I didn't know this when I arrived on campus at the University of Georgia, but soon after pledging a fraternity, one of my brothers in the bonds, Wally Walrus we called him, took me aside and explained the business about the socks.

The way we dressed on Deep South campuses in the sixties was, of course, quite different from the way students dressed at those schools where there was much dissent about all that was traditional. I'm happy the movement did not hit at Georgia until I was out of school; otherwise, I might have had to find a second-hand store to buy myself some blue jeans with patches and an old Army jacket, like the kids were wearing while they were taking over the administration building at Hofstra or some such place as that.

The way we dressed back then, and the way I continued to dress for several years out of school, is now called the "preppie look." This style of dress is yet the target of much derision from those who still don't understand that it does make a difference what sort of animal emblem appears on one's shirt. Some things, I would say to them, are simply the result of good breeding and cannot be explained to anyone who wears Hush Puppies.

I *would* say that, but I won't, because I admit there was a time when I became totally confused about what to wear, and there was a time when I also allowed myself to stray from tradition as far as my clothing was concerned.

I blame all this on Richard Nixon, too. How could one not go off course a bit with all the disillusionment that came with Watergate? It was about the time they caught Nixon up to his ears in justice obstructing that I went out and did something entirely crazy. I bought a new shirt that didn't have any buttons on the collar.

This particular shirt was a dress shirt, and it was sort of a light brown, as I recall. Men not only had started wearing their hair longer, but they also were wearing colorful dress shirts with no buttons on the collars. Since my peers at that point were mostly a bunch of guys who hung around local taverns and belched a lot, I was without any sort of guidance as to what currently was regarded as proper attire for a young man nearing his thirties.

It was about the same time, unfortunately, that the double-knit polyester craze hit full force. I'm not certain who invented double-knit fabrics, but rumor says it was first manufactured in a clothing plant in Fort Deposit, Alabama. This cannot be verified, however, because some years ago a mysterious fire erupted in the warehouse and 26,000 knit leisure suits were destroyed.

The owner, Delbert Gumbatz, was last seen catching the bus to Montgomery. He was wearing a Big Orange leisure suit — a favorite among Tennessee football fans. The last person to see him was the insurance man who signed the check for the fire, which, incidentally, smoldered for nearly six months.

Most everybody was wearing some sort of polyester or double-knit in those days, especially at bowling alleys and Moose Club dances. Such material was so popular, in fact, that several people were severely injured when they were trampled by a mob of shoppers in Good Sam, Ohio, who had just been informed, "Attention, K-Mart shoppers. On aisle seven tonight we have a special on men's leisure suits — all you can haul out of here for $29.95."

After I bought my brown dress shirt with no buttons on the collar, I lost complete control and bought myself a double-knit shirt. It didn't have any buttons on the collar, either, and it featured pictures of exotic-looking birds. To accent this outfit, I also purchased a pair of double-knit trousers. I looked like Marlin Perkins taking the afternoon off from hunting baboons in the wilds of Africa for Mutual of Omaha.

It could have been worse, of course. I could have bought myself a Nehru jacket and one of those medallions on a chain that people who wore Nehru jackets wore around

104

their necks. What stopped me was an experience I had with a friend on the way to lunch one day. He was resplendent in his white Nehru jacket, a pair of white pants, and white patent-leather shoes. His medallion had a picture of Art Garfunkel on it. I was thinking how sharp he looked when three kids stopped him on the street and wanted to buy Eskimo Pies from him. Then two teen-agers thought he was the leader of some religious cult and offered their week's supply of marijuana and asked him to bless their headbands.

I chilled on the Nehru suit.

Later, I considered buying myself a leisure suit, maybe a baby blue one to wear with my Marlin Perkins jungle shirt. I went as far as going into a men's store and asking to see their selection.

"I would like to see a leisure suit," I said to the clerk, who was chewing gum and wearing enough polyester to start his own bingo parlor.

"And what color did we have in mind?" he asked me between chomps on his Juicy Fruit.

"Blue," I said.

"Navy, midnight, morning sky, or baby?" he asked.

"Baby," I said.

He brought out something from the newly-created Tennessee Ernie Ford line, perfect for a night of dining and dancing in the Billy Budd Room at the local Holiday Inn.

"It's you," said the clerk.

"No, it's not," I said. "It's a conventioneer from Nebraska sipping a pina colada and trying to get up the courage to ask a fat girl with a beehive hairdo to dance." I left the store and never considered buying a leisure suit again.

Soon, however, I was once again faced with a dilemma

concerning men's fashions: Would I, or would I not, buy myself a neck chain?

Neck chains were big in singles bars in those days. I suppose that was because women were changing, too, and they had shamelessly indicated that the sight of men's chest hairs made them tingle in places they used to deny they even had, until their husbands pressed them on their wedding nights. So men quit wearing undershirts and started leaving their shirts unbuttoned to their navels, and I suppose neck chains and medallions were a way for men not to feel their chests were totally naked.

I happen to be blessed with a great deal of chest hair, and I readily imagined myself at singles bars covered with young women who wanted to run their fingers through it. So I put on my jungle shirt, buttoned only the bottom button, and went out amongst the night.

Not a single young woman expressed a desire to run her fingers through my chest hair, but I did scare off a dog in the parking lot when he saw my shirt.

I decided a neck chain was what I was missing, so I went the next day to a jewelry store.

"Do you have chains for men?" I asked the clerk.

"You kinky devil," he said.

"I beg your pardon," I replied.

"Didn't mean to insult you," the clerk went on. "I like a little S and M myself occasionally."

"S and M?" I said, completely puzzled.

"Don't kid with me," the clerk said. "We don't have any chains here, but I know where you can get a great deal on whips and leather underwear."

I decided that perhaps I wasn't ready for neck chains just yet. Luckily, however, a friend of mine had just returned

106

from California and had the answer — a string of beads. At first, I was a bit wary of them.

"What's that around your neck?" I asked him.

"Beads," he said. "Everybody in California is wearing beads."

"Isn't that a little, well, sissy?" I asked.

"Get off my back with your macho trip," said my friend. "This is 1974."

Macho. What was this *macho*? Some sort of Mexican dish he had eaten in California? My friend explained.

"What *macho* means," he began, "is a man trying to be like John Wayne all the time — aggressive, insensitive, a slave to old traditions and old hang-ups. If a man wants to make a statement about himself, if he wants to wear a string of beads to say he is caring and sensitive and secure within himself, then he can today without fear of being stereotyped. These beads are my way of saying that I am *laid back,* man."

The entire conversation was far over my head. "Laid back?" I asked.

"Where have you been?" asked my friend. "For years, men have been taught that it's not okay for them to cry, it's not okay for them to enjoy flowers or to dress colorfully or to wear ornamental jewelry. Men who did that were — what was your term? — sissies. Well, we don't have to be like that anymore. Now, we can do our own things. Women really go for guys who can feel, who can share their thoughts, who like poetry and art and antiques and don't mind admitting it. It's even okay for a man to have a cat now."

I was taken aback by all this. True, I had been taught that a man was supposed to be strong and aggressive, and I had always despised cats.

I vowed to change my ways. I borrowed my friend's beads, bought a copy of Kahlil Gibran's *The Prophet,* and took a girl out on a date to the art museum and later to an antique store, where we browsed and looked at brass beds and old pictures of somebody else's grandparents. I thought that was very sensitive of me.

When we reached her house at the end of our date, she said, "I find you so comfortable to be with. You're so sensitive and you don't mind sharing your thoughts. You're so, well, *laid back.*"

I thought I spotted an opening and asked if I could spend the night with her.

"Silly boy," she said. "My cat would be so jealous."

These were trying times for me. With apologies to George Gobel, the world around me seemed to be a tuxedo and I was still a pair of brown shoes.

Leisure suits. Neck chains. Kinky. Macho. Laid back. Men crying and keeping company with cats. Everywhere I looked, there was upheaval and change. And more was on the way.

Women's stated interest in men's chest hairs, which led to the unbuttoned shirts and neck chains and beads, was followed by another shocking admission — they also enjoyed looking at our butts and seeing us in our underpants.

Let's begin with the underpants. The basic rules for men's underpants always had gone something like this:

After a boy-child passes the diaper stage, he moves into what is known as "grippers," or "jockey shorts." These shorts fit very tightly, since small boys have not yet reached the point where tight underwear can cause discomfort and migraine headaches. Before a boy's voice changes, it is perfectly okay for his jockey shorts to have pictures on them, as

108

long as they're pictures of Army tanks or cowboys. Birds and flowers are totally unacceptable.

Once a boy reaches his teens and begins undressing in locker rooms in front of his friends, he still can wear jockey shorts, but forget the pictures of Army tanks and cowboys. Boys at this stage wear plain, white jockey shorts, but they have to be more careful about shorts that fit too snugly because of the aforementioned headaches.

Upon graduation, a young man is fully expected to change into boxer shorts. These shorts are white and they hit just above the knees. A young man should wear this type of undershorts for the remainder of his life, even if he eventually winds up with a truss underneath his clothing, too.

That's the way it used to be, back in a simpler time. Then came Jim Palmer.

Jim Palmer is a famous baseball pitcher who is quite handsome. Some advertising genius got the bright idea to take a picture of Jim Palmer in a pair of bikini-type under-wear for men and put it in a lot of magazines. Men, or should I say those men who do not make a habit of looking at pictures of other men in their underpants, ignored these pictures of Jim Palmer, but women didn't.

They began to say to their mates such things as "Why don't you get some sexy underwear like Jim Palmer wears?"

A lot of men went out and did that, but it posed a real problem for others. What good did it do to wear Jim Palmer underwear if you happened to look like Yogi Berra?

I didn't know what to do. I had a couple of dozen pairs of normal, white boxer shorts, and even walking past a display of Jim Palmer bikini-type underpants made me feel quite silly. My wife at the time insisted, however, that I try out a pair, so I dutifully went into the men's underwear section of a large department store.

Why do they allow women to sell men's underwear?

"Can I help you with something?" asked the girl in the underwear department. I wondered if her father knew she had this job.

"Yes," I mumbled, "I would like to buy some underwear."

"And what type would you like, sir?" she went on.

"Well," I said, "I'm not really certain. Do you have any of those like what's-his-name, the baseball player, wears?"

"Oh, you mean the Jim Palmer jockey brief. Yes, we have all colors in four sizes — Small, Medium, Large, and XLC."

"XLC?"

"Extra Large Crotch," said the salesgirl.

I thought of running out the door. I would never see the salesgirl again, and I could tell my wife that when I got to the department store, there were a lot of fruity-looking characters buying Jim Palmer's underwear and I didn't want to be a part of it.

Before I could make my move, however, the salesgirl was standing in front of me with several pairs of Jim Palmer jockey briefs.

"I can see you're a little unsure, sir," she said. "Why don't you step into our dressing room and try on a pair and see how you like them?"

"Incidentally," I said, "what size are these?"

"Well," said the salesgirl, "it's only a guess, but I picked Small."

When nobody was looking, I slipped out of the dressing room and left my Jim Palmer jockey briefs there. I would explain to my wife that they were all out of my size, and she would understand. She would realize that they probably

110

didn't make many XLC's for guys, well, guys like me.

"All out of Small, huh?" replied my wife.

Jim Palmer was recently released by the Baltimore Orioles and his baseball career is likely over, so I hope he'll put his pants back on and leave the rest of us alone for awhile.

The second part of the problem, as you remember, was that women enjoyed looking at men's butts. They even had calendars with pictures of naked men showing off their buns. This feminine interest in men's hindparts led to another problem regarding the wardrobe, but first some background:

Previous to the revelation that women enjoyed the aesthetic qualities of the male hindpart, men spent little time considering the shape of their hips, much less the presentation of same. They selected a pair of trousers on the basis of comfort alone. Consequently, most men walked around in baggy pants, which offered the ultimate in comfort and free movement, but which also totally veiled the male rear and suggested on some occasions that a family of gypsies had moved out of the seat.

Women's liberation came along, however, and the baggy pants industry went bust, but a boom followed in the blue jean game.

Before, only cowboys and young men under the age of seventeen had worn blue jeans. There was an obvious reason for cowboys' wearing this attire. You can get all sorts of substances on a pair of jeans, like what cows leave all over the dusty trail, and still not have to wash them for weeks at a time ... especially if all the other cowboys' jeans are smelly, too.

Most little boys wanted to be just like the cowboys back then, so their mothers dressed them in jeans. I not only

111

wanted to be a cowboy when I was a child, I was convinced I *was* one. As a matter of fact, I was convinced I was Roy Rogers, who was my favorite western star.

Before we moved to tiny Moreland, we lived in a large apartment complex in Virginia while my father soldiered. I got lost one day. I began to cry. (Cowboys never cry unless they're five and hopelessly lost and hungry and want their mothers.) A kind lady attempted to find out where I lived so she could take me home.

"What's your name, little boy?" she asked.

"Roy Rogers," I said.

She called the resident manager's office and asked where the Rogers family lived. There was no family by that name in the apartment complex.

"Are you certain your name is Roy Rogers?" she asked me again.

"Does Trigger have a long tail?" I asked her back.

Finally, the lady began calling all the apartments asking if anybody had a retarded child who thought he was Roy Rogers. Thankfully, my mother claimed me when the lady reached her.

After high school, a male was expected to step out of his blue jeans and into a pair of baggy pants. It was in this style of dress that he then would leave home for the serious effort of educating himself further, learning a trade, or joining the armed forces, which strenuously objected to any form of tight-fitting trousers since they would deter swift movement on the battlefield.

That has all changed, however. Today, men normally have a closetful of blue jeans, because nothing shows off the hips better than a pair of tight-fitting blue jeans, and they're considered appropriate attire for practically every occasion

112

except state funerals.

Most men, raised under the old rules of loose-fitting pants, had to learn a number of new rules about buying jeans:

1. They had to remember to buy their jeans at least two inches smaller in the waist than the jeans and trousers they bought before Women's Liberation. Some jeans advertised a "skosh" more room in the seat, but I don't think they sold very well. That one little "skosh" just might be enough to cause you to go unnoticed by a gaggle of gimlet-eyed legal secretaries hip-watching during a Friday afternoon happy hour.

2. They had to remember that if they decided to bend over for any reason while wearing tight-fitting jeans, they should take a deep breath first to avoid passing out. Rule 2-A is, if you bend over and hear a ripping sound, place both hands over your backside and run backwards towards the nearest restroom. At an outdoor function, cover and run backwards towards the nearest heavy growth of kudzu.

3. It was important to note that tight-fitting jeans could be the devil to remove from your body. Men had to remember always to carry a pocketknife with them when they were wearing their tight jeans, just in case it became necessary to cut them away from their bodies in an extreme emergency ... such as if they were sick and tired of sleeping in them.

4. Men had to accept the fact that while they were wearing tight jeans, they absolutely had to hold their stomachs in at all times, even though doing so would cause their faces to turn red and their eyes to bug out (not to mention the possibility of swollen ankles).

It was in the late seventies that I finally relented and went out and bought my first pair of adult blue jeans. I was surprised at the varieties available. Even the noted snooty designers Bill Blass and Calvin Klein had jeans lines, which suddenly cost what a man used to pay for a Sunday suit.

I bought myself a pair of tight-fitting Kleins and wore them out of the store and headed to the nearest singles bar. I ordered a drink and made certain I kept my backside pointed toward the tables of legal secretaries sipping pina coladas, figuring the sight of my new jeans hugging closely to my hips would knock the umbrellas right out of their glasses.

Unfortunately, no action was forthcoming. A man standing next to me in a pair of tight-fitting Bill Blass jeans finally turned to me and said, "How long you been here?"

"Couple of beers," I answered.

"Me, too," he replied. "I don't think I've gotten one glance."

There was something terribly wrong here. We had both spent half a week's salary on a pair of designer jeans that we had stuffed ourselves into, and all the women who were supposed to go wild at the sight of men's hips hadn't shown the slightest interest.

"I guess it's like my old grandpa used to say," said Bill Blass. " 'It don't matter what kind of rifle you have if you ain't got any ammunition to load it with.' "

I finished my beer, went home, and cut myself out of my Calvin Klein jeans. I spent the remainder of the evening attempting to learn to breathe normally again.

* * *

I have never ceased to be amazed by the lengths men will go to satisfy a feminine whim. Take aftershave lotion. God

114

gave men Old Spice aftershave lotion, and that should have been enough. But, no. Women decided that Old Spice, which is what everybody's daddy wore, wasn't nearly the sexy aroma they wanted, and so men had another problem — What sort of aftershave should I use to set my woman's blood to boiling?

There was English Leather. You know what the sexy lady on television says about that — "My men wear English Leather ... or they wear nothing at all."

I can just see it now. I go over to have dinner with her and her parents, and I show up naked as a jaybird.

"Are you crazy?" she screams at me.

"Well," I attempt to explain, "I was all out of English Leather and the stores were closed, so like you say, either I wear English Leather or I wear...."

Somebody later figured out that what a woman really wanted to smell on a man was his natural odor with a little perfume thrown in. The upshoot of that revelation was something called "musk." I could never bring myself to splash anything called "musk" all over my face. It sounded too much like the way it smelled in the kitchen after I hadn't taken the garbage out for a week.

Pete Rose tried to get us back on track and away from all those exotic perfumed potions when he claimed "a man wants to smell like a man" and urged us all to buy Aqua Velva, first cousin to Old Spice. Of course, with Pete Rose's money, he could splash tobacco juice on his face and still make out.

The big question facing men today is, if I use Paco Rabanne cologne, will I score as much as the guys in their advertisements obviously do?

I never have actually smelled Paco Rabanne, but their

ads, which also appear in a number of women's magazines because women are the ones who buy most of the cosmetics for men in the first place, are something else.

Get the picture: This muscular fellow is in bed and covers are all askew. It's obvious that the only thing between him and butt-naked is the sheet he has pulled up just enough to avoid embarrassing his parents, in case they happened to stumble across the ad.

He's on the telephone, talking to the woman who spent the night with him but who had to get up early for an appointment with the board of directors. She is a totally New Woman, who doesn't want children until she has been made a partner in the firm. She also is very open about her sexuality, which means she always carries an extra toothbrush in her handbag just in case.

In a Paco Rabanne ad, you read the dialogue between the man naked in the bed and the woman on the other end of the telephone. It goes something like this:

WOMAN: "You animal."

MAN: "I was just thinking about you."

WOMAN: "You beast."

MAN: "So it was good for you. I was embarrassed to ask."

WOMAN: "My toes are still tingling."

MAN: "Down, girl."

WOMAN: "What are you doing right now?"

MAN: "I'm naked under the sheets."

WOMAN: "You devil."

MAN: "Are you coming back over tonight?"

WOMAN: "Can Burl Ives sell tea?"

MAN: "I'll splash on a lot of Paco Rabanne."

WOMAN: "Forget my career. Forget my partnership in the firm. I'll be right over."

116

MAN: "Sure you don't mind?"

WOMAN: "My mind might not be sure, you hunk, but the rest of me is."

Paco Rabanne for men. What is remembered is up to you.

How are men supposed to stick to something simple like Old Spice when they can pop for a little Paco Rabanne and maybe stay naked under the sheets for weeks at a time?

Sex. It's everywhere. It's in the music, it determines what clothes we wear, and even what we splash on our faces after we shave.

Do we really have it better than our parents? Sex was simple for them. All they had to do was memorize one position and remember to turn the light off.

But sex has been a whole new ball game for my generation. I'm still not certain if a *ménage à trois* is some sort of French cooking with lots of sauce or something you do naked under the sheets with a girls' volleyball team. And with my luck, about the time I find out, I'll have ulcers and will be too old for it to really matter.

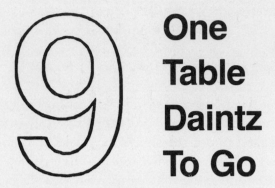

9 One Table Daintz To Go

SEX TODAY IS just as scrambled as everything else. You can't even talk about it without getting confused. As evidence, I present a glossary of modern sexual terms:

— LOVER: Somebody you aren't married to, but you're sleeping with them anyway.

— COHABITATION: When your lover moves into your apartment and brings all of his or her clothes and starts getting his or her mail at your address. You still aren't married but you're telling your parents that any day now you will be.

— PALIMONY: What you have to pay your ex-lover monthly, even though you never did get around to marrying her.

— GAY: Formerly "queer," "fruit," or "fag." Means you and your lover can go into the same bathroom together when you stop at service stations during long trips.

— AIDS: You and your lover can share the same hospital room together, too.

— PLATO'S RETREAT: Club in New York City where anything goes, including having sex with any number of total strangers.

— HERPES: A little something to remember your last night at Plato's Retreat by.

— RELATIONSHIP: What you tell your friends you're having with your boss because "affair" sounds so tacky.

— G-SPOT: When you touch a woman there, she makes very loud noises. The next morning the kids want to know if there was a panther in your bedroom last night.

— HUNK: What women call exceptionally attractive men.

— RICHARD GERE: Hollywood hunk who has never appeared with his shirt on for more than two minutes at a time in any of his movies.

— BATTERY STOCKS: Really have nothing to do with sex, but have you noticed how much they've gone up since modern women discovered vibrators may be used for more than soothing the tired feet they used to get from standing at the ironing board?

— *PENTHOUSE* MAGAZINE FORUM: Where readers write in to tell of their unusual sexual experiences. Many of these experiences are totally sick and perverted, and the magazine is nothing more than a blight on public decency. Nice people would never be caught reading such trash.

— *PENTHOUSE* MAGAZINE CIRCULATION: It's somewhere in the millions.

— X-RATED: Movie industry rating for film that includes explicit sex scenes.

— R-RATED: Movie industry rating for film that includes explicit sex scenes, but there is some semblance of a plot.

— PG-RATED: Movie industry rating for film where the

119

sex scenes are not quite as steamy, the plot may actually make sense, and your parents won't be totally embarrassed to watch it.

— *PLAYBOY* CHANNEL: Cable television channel that features X-rated films in your very own home and usually shows the most explicit sex scenes after your parents are asleep. The sound tracks on these films are optional, so there's no need to turn up the volume and risk awakening your parents.

— THE POPE: Powerful religious figure who recently said sex is sinful unless it's being performed for the strict purpose of procreation.

— JERRY FALWELL: Another powerful religious figure who would like to see sex done away with altogether, but he hasn't been able to come up with a viable alternative.

— JOGGING, RACQUETBALL, PLAYING *TRIVIAL PURSUIT,* AND BACKGAMMON: A few activities that have failed miserably as alternatives to sex, but people keep trying them anyway.

— S AND M: Odd sexual activity, involving whips and black leather outfits, which may be traced back to former cowboy star Lash Larue.

— KINKY: Sexual behavior involving the use of duck feathers.

— PERVERTED: You use the whole duck.

See what I mean? That's why so many sex manuals make it to the bestseller list and why the argument for sex education classes in our schools is such a good one. Perhaps if we teach our children all about sex in the schools, then they will be able to explain it to their parents.

We really didn't need sex education classes when I was in

school, because there wasn't that much to learn. You could get about all the sexual knowledge that was known at the time from an older classmate in a very short period of time ... say, just as long as it took for an older classmate to explain that all you'll ever find in a cabbage patch is cabbage and maybe a rat snake or two.

I'm not certain when sex became so confusing, but I think it was when women decided to take part in it. Frankly, I don't blame them for that, because sex — with the afore-mentioned exception of when you're sunburned and also when you're very sleepy or there's a ball game on you want to watch — can be quite a rewarding experience.

But previously, only men had sex. Women were there when all this was taking place, but theirs was basically the role of a waitress who puts the food on the table and says, "I hope you enjoy it," and then goes back to the kitchen to have a smoke.

I suspect that it was a man who got women involved in sex. It probably was the first man who made love to a woman and then wondered if it had been as pleasant for her as it had been for him, so he asked that infamous question: "Was it good for you?"

Men had never wondered that before. You didn't ask your bird dog how he enjoyed the hunting trip or your fishing worm how the water was.

I suppose our previous attitude came from the puritanical belief that sex was basically a rotten thing to do, and if a woman took some pleasure from the experience, she obviously was not the delicate flower she was supposed to be and should be tied to the dunking stool. It took women three hundred years to get over the fear that if they uttered one little sound of pleasure during sex or actually moved, they would be severely punished. I'm not certain, however, if what they feared most was the embarrassment of being dunked in public or the horror of getting their hair wet.

So when the first man asked the question, "Was it good for you?", he created a real dilemma for the woman.

If it *hadn't* been good for her and she admitted it, women's sexual liberation would have been set back another three hundred years, because her sexual partner would have gone out and told all his friends, "Aha! It's just as we expected. They really don't have any fun when they have sex."

But if she *had* enjoyed it and she said so, that same creep would have gone out and told all his friends that she was some sort of brazen hussy who actually enjoyed sex. By the time the gossip got around, the rumor would be that she had said she not only enjoyed sex but often spent ten or fifteen minutes a day thinking about it, and that kind of rumor could get you kicked out of the Junior League.

I admire that first woman who admitted she had, in fact, thoroughly enjoyed the experience of sex. It might have gone something like this:

"Sweetheart?"

"Yes, my dear?"

"May I ask you a question?"

"You want me to run to the store to get you a pack of cigarettes?"

"No, not at all. I just want to ask you a question."

"I really don't mind going to the store. I don't have to start dinner for another half hour."

"That's not it at all, sweetheart. There's just something that has been on my mind."

"You're wondering whether or not I would mind if you went bowling Friday night and then stayed out and had a few beers with the boys and came in all sloppy drunk and passed out in the floor of the living room. Of course, I don't mind, dear. I know you need some time of your own."

"That's not it at all, Sugar Love. See, some of the guys down at the plant and me were talking and this one guy wanted to know, well...."

"If I would bring my delicious brownies to the union hall for next week's meeting?"

"No, he wanted to know, uh, he just wondered if women enjoyed sex, too."

"Marvin!"

"No, Lovey, I mean it's something guys think about a lot. I mean, was what we just did, I mean, you know ... was it good for you?"

"It was great."

"It was?"

"I loved it."

"You're kidding me."

"No, I'm not. It was absolutely wonderful and let's do it again right now."

"I can't right now, Honey. I've got to run down to the plant and tell the other guys."

You can see the trouble this started. Marvin told the other guys, and then they asked their wives, and their wives said they enjoyed sex, too, and soon the word got out all over. Suddenly women all over the world were no longer ashamed to admit their interest in lovemaking, and that's how the sexual revolution began.

The sexual revolution may have liberated women sexually, but it put a great deal of heretofore unfelt pressure on men. Sometime after the first publication of *Playgirl* magazine, where handsome men posed nude for the now-accepted prurient interests of women, women not only were admitting to men that they enjoyed sex, but they were answering the was-it-good-for-you question honestly. Men never have been the same sexually since.

"Sweetheart?"

"Yes, Marvin."

"Was it good for you?"

"Want to know the truth?"

"Of course, my sweet."

"No."

"Do what?"

"It wasn't good for me at all. In a recent article in *Cosmopolitan,* eight out of every ten women polled said their sexual partners did not engage in enough foreplay, were not sensitive enough to the female's needs, and insisted the lights be turned off."

"How would you have voted in that poll, my pet?"

"Turn on the lights, Speedy Gonzales, and I'll show you my ballot."

After this, of course, men had to take special care to please their sexual partners, and this was not an easy thing for them to do because of their backgrounds, and because very few of them read *Cosmo.*

This pressure also resulted in some men suffering from impotence and in the eventual creation of ESPN, the twenty-four-hour all-sports cable television network, which gives men something to do at night after their sexual partners have begun holding up rating cards like judges at diving meets. This, of course, eventually causes them to be too nervous to do anything but watch rodeos and college hockey games on the tube until three in the morning.

The sexual revolution and the revelation that women

124

actually enjoyed being part of the sexual experience also sent sex into a fad stage, where it remains to this day.

Having simple sex isn't enough anymore. The various sex manuals have revealed there are many kinky positions in which to have sex, such as with your favorite shortstop in the dirt part of the infield so you won't get all scratched up on the artificial turf, and there are all sorts of extracurricular activities that may be interwoven with the sex act.

Today's trendy magazines are filled with examples and instructions regarding such matters. Read the *Penthouse* Forum, for example, and you will wonder if you're the only person left alive on earth who hasn't had sex while riding in a Ferris wheel or standing on your head at a Tupperware party.

It seems that something new and confusing comes out everyday with regard to sex.

And for somebody like me, who was reared in the sexual naiveté of the fifties and who always had a great deal of trouble understanding and getting along with women in the first place, the entire sexual scene has become totally baffling and frustrating.

I'm not certain how I should act around women anymore in order to attract their attention or to arouse any sort of physical interest in me.

I've tried to be sensitive at times by pouring my beer into a glass before I drink it, but all this usually gets me is a long discussion about how her ex-husband used to make love with his socks on.

I've also tried to be like Clint Eastwood and stare at her with my cold yet lusty eyes and not say very much, but all this usually leads to is my being terribly uncomfortable. I mean, sooner or later a man needs to go to the bathroom, but you never saw Clint Eastwood putting the move on a beautiful woman and suddenly announcing that he had to go to the bathroom. He's much too cool for that. Of course, the reason he's always clenching his teeth and has that stern look about him is that he hasn't been to the bathroom in a week, and it's killing him.

I never know what to say to girls in bars anymore, either. Bogart and those guys used to walk over to a woman, light her cigarette, and say, "Sweetheart, where have you been all my life?" and that was it. My generation countered with, "What's your sign?" and "I hate to see anybody drink alone," but then women wised up to those. Now, I think the only men who ever meet women in bars and something actually comes of it are those weirdos who write to *Penthouse* Forum:

"I'm twenty-three and quite a handsome guy, if I do say so myself, and let me tell you what happened to me one recent night when I was on a business trip to Toledo.

"I walked into a bar and there was this gorgeous blonde, wearing a tight-fitting pink sweater and black leather pants and roller skates, standing alone nursing a pina colada.

"I took a spot next to her at the bar and ordered myself a gin and Pepsi. She took off her Sony Walkman and skated closer to me. I could feel her hot breath with the faint scent of coconut against my flushed face.

"We finished our drinks, and without saying a word, this voluptuous creature and I walked (she skated) out of the bar and went back to my hotel room.

"I have never spent such a night of ecstasy. She took off all my clothes and tied me to the bed with a rope she carried in her handbag, and then she skated up and down on me until I was driven out of my mind with passion.

126

"The next morning, my back looked like they had run the Indy 500 time trials on it, but I will never forget the gorgeous blonde at the bar, and now every time I see Roller Derby on television, I'm aroused. I would be interested to know if any of your other readers have ever had such an experience."

Not me, although a girl did nearly run me down on her Harley one afternoon outside a bowling alley in Houston.

Women are simply too sexually aware today for anybody to sweep them off their feet, especially in a bar where they dress seductively and go to see how many men they can reduce to sniveling idiots. It has been my experience that such women especially enjoy making vulnerable, recently-divorced men feel as though they need to go back immediately and crawl under the rock from which they obviously sprang. This story requires a little background:

I got one of my divorces when I was living in Chicago. I distinctly remember the conversation with my wife when I first learned that she was terribly unhappy being married to me. I called home one evening from work.

"Hi, sweetheart," I began. "What's for dinner?"

"What did you do for dinner before you got married?"

"What kind of question is that?"

"A perfectly good question. What did you do for dinner before you got married?"

"Ate a lot of fish sticks. Why?"

"Here's a hint: Frozen fish sticks are on sale at the Jewell Store. I'd advise you to stop there on your way home."

That was just her funny way of saying she was splitting.

Years later, I figured the whole thing out. Being a house-wife had caused her to lose her identity, and what she

needed was to find her own space and establish a relationship with someone who didn't mind preparing fish
sticks for *her* once in a while.

At the time, however, I was yet languishing in the idea that
it should be enough for a woman that I worked hard and
provided for her and didn't talk ugly about her kinfolks.
That belief I had picked up from role models during my
youth. The old people at home would talk about marriage
and the duties of the partners in such conversations as this:

"Heard Clovis Niles is gettin' married."

"Who to?"

"Grover Turnipseed."

"He's a fine boy."

"Don't drink much."

"Works hard, too."

"Don't lay out in beer joints all night."

"Owns his own double-wide trailer."

"He'll make a good provider."

"She's a good cook."

"Sews, too."

"And cans."

In the seventies, of course, women began to want a lot
more than a man who owned his own double-wide, but
somehow I missed that announcement. So there I was, stuck
in Chicago, the snows of winter just around the end-of-
October corner, my wife gone, and fish sticks up to my ears.

I had very little luck getting dates in Chicago after my
wife left. The biggest problem was that when I went into
singles bars on Division Street, I usually was confronted by a
lot of people wearing huge furry coats and hats and gloves
— they were still trying to thaw out from the cold on the
sidewalks outside. (Chicago is the coldest place on earth

where polar bears don't roam free.)

The drawback to all that cold-weather gear was that it was often difficult to determine male from female. Everybody looks basically alike when they're dressed like Nanook of the North. That's why Eskimos spend a lot of time cutting holes in the ice and fishing — it's safer than making the wrong move in the igloo and winding up putting the make on the guy with whom you share your kayak.

My next problem, once I had distinguished the men from the women, was my previously admitted inability to think of anything clever to say to a total stranger in a bar. This problem was amplified by the fact that Chicago women — know affectionately as "Michigan Avenue Marauders" — were anything but gentle to poor souls like myself, who were simply looking for someone with whom to huddle against the cold.

Imagine this scene: I'm lonely and far from home. My wife has split and I'm crawling all over thirty, and whatever speed I once had on my singles bar fastball is now only a memory. But a man has to try. A man simply has to try.

She's sitting there on a stool at the bar at Butch McGuire's, and for some girl who's probably from Indiana and works for an advertising firm, she's not bad at all. (She could have been from North Dakota and pumped gas, for all I cared at the time.)

"Gee, it's cold outside," I used as an ice-breaker, if you will.

"What was your first clue, Dick Tracy?"

"That's cute. Could I buy you a drink?"

"Suit yourself."

"What will you have?"

"Cutty rocks."

129

"Cutty rocks, bartender. I like these Irish bars, don't you?"

"They're okay. Except you have to talk to a lot of weirdos."

"Speaking of Irishmen, hear the one about the two Irish gays?"

"No, but I get the feeling I'm going to."

"Yeah, there was Michael Fitzpatrick and Patrick Fitzmichael. Get it?"

"Thanks for the drink, Tex. I gotta catch the train to Skokie."

There was one night in Butch's when I thought I finally had scored. She was a lovely thing, standing over at the corner of the bar. Just to be sure, I looked down at her feet. She was wearing pink galoshes. Normally, the men in Chicago, even the strange ones, don't wear pink galoshes.

She was staring at me. I was certain of it. I continued to glance over at her. Each time our eyes met, she smiled. This was it! All I had to do was walk over, introduce myself, hit her with a few quick stories, and I would be in.

I didn't want to rush it, however. I ordered myself another drink, casually lit a cigarette, blew out a couple of perfectly-formed smoke rings, and tried to look slightly bored, so that when I said to her, "I really hate these kinds of places; they're nothing but meat markets," she would not doubt my sincerity.

When I thought the time was right, I strolled toward her. Her eyes were still staring directly into mine, her lips curved in a knowing smile.

"I really hate these kinds of places; they're nothing but meat markets," I began.

"I hope you don't mind if I tell you something," the lady said.

130

"I know you don't usually come on to men like this," I replied, trying to make her feel at ease with her obvious advances. "But don't feel bad about it. It's okay for a woman to do things like that today. We aren't living in the Stone Age anymore, you know."

That would do it, of course. She would recognize me as a very aware person — sensitive, caring, with a beast inside me somewhere, just waiting for the right woman to come along and awaken it.

"I don't want to embarrass you," the woman said, "but your fly is open."

I went back to my apartment, crawled under the bed, assumed the fetal position, and had a nervous breakdown.

* * *

One of the things militant feminists say about men is that we feel threatened by the new feminine aggressiveness and assertiveness. They're right, especially when they say things like that about men who remember women the way they used to be.

We're terribly confused about what women want us to do, when they want us to do it, and for how long. And we aren't certain that one day they aren't going to ditch us altogether, when somebody invents a computer that can do about three or four things at once with the proper mixture of tenderness and boldness, and after women are finished using it, it won't roll over and snore and keep them awake all night.

Do you know what's making a comeback in this country on the sex front? Strip joints, that's what. Strip joints are making a comeback because men can go in there an ogle and whistle and make all those remarks they learned in the

131

Navy, and the women won't get angry and call their sisters-in-arms and cause the men all sorts of embarrassment and bodily pain.

I wandered into a place one night in Memphis called The Yellow Pussycat. All around me were young women. They were quite naked and they were dancing. I ordered myself a drink and began to watch. Soon, I was approached by one of the young women who had been dancing.

"Wanta table daintz?" she asked. ("Daintz" is the way "dance" comes out when a naked Southern girl with a mouthful of gum says it.)

"What's a table dance?" I asked.

She rolled her eyes as if to ponder what primitive means of transportation recently had dropped me at this address.

"You pay me seven dollars," she said, "and I daintz on your table."

"A sort of private dance, huh?" I probed.

She rolled her eyes again. "Others can watch if they want to," she explained, "but they won't get to see nothin' up close like you will."

Good sport that I am, I paid the seven bucks and experienced my first table dance. The problem was that I am easily embarrassed and often feel quite self-conscious in public, and here I was — a total stranger in a place that obviously wasn't the Christian Science Reading Room, and a young woman I never had seen before in my life was dancing on my table, often moving close enough for me to see the innermost construction of her navel.

I didn't want to stare directly at her and appear like some old lecher, but on the other hand, I had paid the seven bucks and felt obliged to get my money's worth by watching every twitch and strut.

132

Had we been sipping wine alone together and Table Daintzer had suddenly been so moved by the music and the passion and the subsequent giddiness that she had climbed atop a nearby table to disrobe and move sensuously to the music, I would have thoroughly enjoyed the experience. In this setting, however, I was more than uncomfortable.

After the table dance was mercifully over, she asked me if I wanted another, and I said, "Thank you, but no." Then she said that if I would buy her a bottle of champagne (she split the cost with the house twenty-eighty, she explained, and needed the money in order to pay for her little sister's operation), she would join me at my table and we could talk.

Naturally, I wanted to help all I could with her little sister's operation, so I ordered the champagne and we sat and talked. It was the first time I had had a conversation with a woman in years that we didn't have to discuss her career.

I admit openly and without shame that I am intimidated by today's modern woman. The female role models I had as a child were my mother, who still made homemade biscuits in the morning, and my teachers, who were too busy teaching me how to long divide to tell me that when I grew up, women would be drinking and smoking and sweating in public and telling dirty jokes and would punch you in the mouth if you made a remark they deemed sexist.

Women didn't sweat, or at least I didn't think they did, until the late sixties. I went to school with little girls who wore sundresses and thought it terribly unfeminine to engage in any sort of activity that might indicate they hadn't been born with their sweat glands nailed completely shut, so they could grow up to be cheerleaders and could lift their hands to clap and not be concerned that somebody would see wet spots under their arms. There was even the axiom that "horses sweat, men perspire, and women *glow.*"

That didn't change in college, either. The girls there wore cute little outfits and were in school to find husbands. The only ones who were in school to learn anything were the ones who wore thick glasses and played horn. They all eventually grew up to become militant feminists, of course, and they're getting back at us now for all those years the rest of us were busy having parties and picking mates, while they were down at the music room blowing into a stupid trumpet or tuba. The fact that most militant feminists wear thick glasses and have pooched-out lips from too many nights of blowing into horns is proof of my contention.

It was sweat, I think, that finally led to most women's casting aside their previous role as demure little things, to be left in the kitchen while the men withdrew to the study for cigars and brandy to discuss the pros and cons of the designated hitter.

I saw it coming in 1968. The University of Georgia at that time was intent on keeping passion to a minimum on campus. The free-sex movement had started on some Northern campuses, but at Georgia, students had remained in the political and moral status quo. Once you gave a girl your fraternity pin, you might expect a little something more than a kiss goodnight — especially if Georgia had won its football game that week — but nobody ever was late for botany class because they had lost track of the time during a heated moment of noonday passion.

One of the ways the university attempted to keep the status quo was by not allowing coeds to walk around campus in their gym shorts after P.E. classes, thus tempting male students.

134

For years coeds never muttered a sound about this rule. After P.E., they simply put their raincoats around their gym outfits and went to their next class. They never complained in hot weather, of course, because since *ladies* didn't sweat and smell gamey, walking around in a raincoat didn't bother them, even if they had just completed a rousing game of volleyball and the temperature was over ninety degrees.

In the spring of 1968, however, a young coed named DeLores Perkwater, who wore thick glasses and played horn, passed out in class from heat exposure following her gym session. When they took her raincoat off, they noticed she was perspiring profusely.

Even the more demure coeds from the finest sororities subsequently decided that making them wear raincoats after gym class was cruel and unusual punishment, and the first notice I had of what was to come in the feminist movement occurred soon after. A number of slogan-chanting Georgia coeds, marching in the name of DeLores Perkwater, took over the administration building and refused to leave until the university rescinded the gym shorts rule.

Officials might have won out, but the protest took place late in spring quarter, and after the coeds had been inside the administration building (which was not air-conditioned at the time) for several days without benefit of bathing, the atmosphere became so pungent that the university decided to give in.

"Coeds Free To Sweat!" screamed the headlines in the school newspaper, and soon women all over the country began sweating in public and thinking nothing of it. This eventually led women to begin exercising, building their bodies, and applying for jobs as construction workers and goat ropers and all sorts of other jobs previously performed

135

by men only.

Once women began to do all that, there was no stopping them. And they owe it all to DeLores Perkwater, now commander of the 14th Bomber Wing of the National Organization of Women.

* * *

I'm not certain what my own future will be regarding women. I am currently single, and I don't know what sort of woman I would want to marry if ever I married again.

I still would like to have a wife who cooks a meal occasionally, even if she happens to be the governor. I still like women who don't know everything that I know, so I can tell them something occasionally and they can look at me like I'm quite intelligent. In other words, I want a woman who I stand at least an even chance at beating in a game of *Trivial Pursuit* and who doesn't understand the infield fly rule, so I can take her to baseball games and put my arm around her and say things like, "Well, sweetheart, it's like this...."

I do not want a woman who has hairy legs like mine. I don't want a woman who is in any shape or form involved in the martial arts, and I don't want a woman who comes to bed smelling like a can of Penzoil because her hobby is rebuilding race cars for the Junior Johnson racing team.

I don't want a woman who introduces me to all sorts of strange sexual techniques that she picked up on a recent business trip to the Orient. I don't want a woman who knees me in the belly when I forget to put the top back on the toothpaste, and I don't want a woman who gets into drinking bouts with Marine recruits and maintains a winning percentage.

136

It's the same old problem for me: I want a woman like women were in 1962, because I remember them as being soft and nice to hold and, like Merle Haggard said, they could still cook back then and still would. I don't mind if girls grow up to be president these days, and I don't think women should be given smaller wages simply because they're women, but what do I do with these old-fashioned feelings that were instilled in me? What can I do about the fact that a woman in a coat and tie carrying a briefcase doesn't do much for me in the area of physical attraction? I didn't come here to take out a loan, madam, I wanted to hug you and kiss you on your mouth.

What I'm doing here is dilly-dallying around. I know exactly what I want in a woman.

I want a woman who was raised in a rural atmosphere and whose mother taught her to bake pies and fry chicken and make gravy and iced tea.

I want her to have no ambition beyond making me very happy and comfortable, including giving me back rubs at night and not complaining when I keep the television on until two in the morning watching a ball game from the West Coast.

I want her to be good to my dog, and I want her to take her own overheads when we play tennis and to lob when I tell her to. I want her to be open and willing sexually, but I don't want her to insist on anything acrobatic that could cause me to have a back injury or get an eye put out.

I want her to like country music and at least understand the basics of college football as it is played in major conferences, and I want her to make devilled eggs to carry to the games for the pre-game brunch, and if it happens to rain, I don't want to hear, "How much longer is this thing going to last?"

I want her to pop me popcorn on cold nights when we're sitting in front of the fire. I want her to make certain there always is cold beer in the ice box and that I never run out of clean underwear. I want her to talk sweetly to me on mornings after I've made a fool out of myself at a party and have a terrible hangover, and I want her to be afraid of spiders and call me to come squish them when she sees one running across the floor in the kitchen.

The sad truth is that I have known and have had such women, but for one reason or other, I have let them get away. I'm not certain there are very many like them left, and it probably would serve me right if I wound up with DeLores Perkwater.

In the midst of this dilemma, I always harken back to the words of my boyhood friend and idol, Weyman C. Wannamaker, Jr., a great American, who once surveyed the changing scene of the roles for women and said, "The whole thing boils down to the fact that the opposite sex ain't nearly as opposite as it used to be."

To further complicate the matter of sex in the 1980s, of course, we are a society attempting to deal with the gay movement. I cannot quote Weyman on his thoughts regarding the gay movement, because he is not at all tolerant in that area. Okay, maybe just one quote:

"All you hear about these days," says Weyman, "is them queers (I'm sorry, but Weyman refuses to say *gay* and it took me months to get him to tone it down to *queer*) and how they have all come out of the closet. I'll tell you one thing — I bet it was a mess in that closet when they were all back up in there together."

Weyman's basic problem with the gay movement, and

mine as well, is that we have had no background whatsoever in dealing with something that seems quite unnatural, occasionally appalling, and, even in my most tolerant moments, something that I one day might be able to accept but never understand.

As far as I know, the first gay person I ever saw was a waiter in a spiffy Atlanta restaurant. I'm not certain why, but it seems there is an overabundant number of effeminate young men working in spiffy restaurants these days. Now, I understand that just because a male is effeminate, it doesn't necessarily mean that he's gay, and just because a man may come on as a rugged, macho-type, it doesn't necessarily mean that he's straight. However (and I promise this is the last time I'm going to quote Weyman on such a sensitive issue), when I see a young man sashay over to me in a spiffy restaurant, and he just sort of floats when he walks and he's what we used to call prissy, I cannot help but harken back to what Weyman says when he sees somebody like that: "Damn, but if I don't believe that ol' boy's about half-queer."

Anyway, some years ago I went into a restaurant, and a young man fitting the above description prissed over to my table and said in a delicate voice, "Hi, I'm Keith, and I'll be your waiter this evening." He sort of put a question mark on the end of "evening," ending his pronouncement with a bit of a wrist movement that you never see from the grill man at an all-night truckstop.

I didn't know exactly what to say, so I said, "Hi there, Keith, I'm Lewis and I'll be your customer."

All that straight, he began by telling me and my party about what *wasn't* on the menu. (I don't know why spiffy restaurants never put their good stuff on the menu, but they don't.)

139

"Tonight," said Keith, "we have some absolutely *sker-rump-tious* specials."

With that, he delivered an entire litany of dishes I had never heard of. When I said I'd just have the ground sirloin steak, well done, and some fries, he looked at me with a beady-eyed smirk as if to say, "How on earth did someone so uncivilized find my table?"

I think that's what I dislike most about going into an overpriced restaurant and having to deal with gay waiters: If you don't order something that sounds like it ought to have a part in a film with subtitles, gay waiters look at you like you've just broken wind. I try never to break wind in a restaurant, which is why I never order anything that might start my gastronomic network into embarrassing emissions.

There weren't any gay people in Moreland when I was growing up. We thought there was one once, and that led to months of gossip and suspense, but it turned out to be a false alarm.

There was this kid named Donnelle Spinks, who was about my age. His mother named him after his great aunt Donnelle, because he was her eighth and final child and she already had produced seven boys, all ugly and quite useless, and she had prayed for a girl. When Donnelle was born and turned out to be quite male, she figured she would simply make up for the Lord's obvious mistake.

She dressed Donnelle in girl's clothes until he started school and put ribbons in his hair and bought him dolls, and she would have taught him to sew and given him piano lessons had Mr. Spinks not eventually put his foot down. Donnelle, however, had to face terrible abuse from his classmates because of his name and the way he walked — it was aptly described as walking like he was trying to carry a

140

corncob in his crack.

Donnelle also had a rather effeminate voice with a slight lisp, and when it was discovered during a recess baseball game that his throw back to the cut-off man in the infield was delivered with the wristy technique of a girl, he was further branded as "queer as a rooster that wouldn't set foot in the henhouse."

Donnelle took the blows and the nasty comments until one afternoon in the sixth grade, when Alvin Bates, a smart-aleck teacher's pet, began to chide him on the playground near where the second graders were swinging on the monkey bars.

"Hey, Donelle," said Alvin, "your mother still puttin' dresses on you?"

Donnelle was used to this sort of thing, of course. He continued to do what he always did when somebody started the queer business with him — he ignored Alvin.

But then Alvin got nasty. "Hey, Donnelle," he said, "you going to play dolls after school today?"

Donnelle was still ignoring Alvin, who hadn't had enough.

"Hey, Donnelle, you a boy or a girl?"

"Quit picking on him, Alvin," said Betty Ann Hillback, who had performed a duet with Donnelle in the piano class recital.

"What's he going to do about it, Betty Ann?" asked Alvin. "Why don't you go hide in a closet and improve the scenery around here?"

Suddenly, unexpectedly, Donnelle was walking towards Alvin. "You can't talk to her that way," he said.

"What're you going to do about it, queer boy?" Alvin replied.

Betty Ann, the nervous type, had begun to cry.

"Tell her you're sorry for saying that," Donnelle demanded of Alvin.

"Who's going to make me?"

"Tell her."

"Kiss my...."

It all happened so quickly. Donnelle pounced on Alvin and inflicted facial wounds by the dozens. Donnelle then dragged Alvin over to the monkey bars, doubled him over one, and began giving him a series of quick kicks to his rear. Alvin soon was more than ready to apologize to Betty Ann for his insult.

Later, Alvin told the teacher that Donnelle Spinks had beaten him up, and the teacher called Mr. Spinks in to discuss the violent behavior of his son.

They say that after Mr. Spinks found out Donnelle had severely thrashed another boy on the school playground, he and his son became much closer, and Mr. Spinks bought Mrs. Spinks a little poodle dog, so she would still have something to pet now that Donnelle had become Don and had taken up the habit of walking to church with Betty Ann Hillback and holding her hand. That's when we knew for sure that Donnelle wasn't gay.

Today, I have too much trouble dealing with my own problems in the area of sexual relations to spend a great deal of time being concerned with those of others. That's why if someone chooses to be gay — or can't help it — that's fine with me ... as long as they don't attempt to do whatever gay people do near where I'm eating, watching a movie or a ball game, or attempting to fish, because such antics can be terribly distracting.

I would suggest that if gay people — who seem to have

142

become more and more vocal and more prone to displays of public affection as their numbers and acceptance into the mainstream have grown — have the sudden urge to love on one another and they can't find a motel room or the back-seat of a car parked off in the woods somewhere, they should go back into the closet. It won't be for long, and they can come right back out when they're done.

I also am against gay people as a political force, because it's not wise to mix sex and politics. Had our forefathers known what was going to happen to American sex, they likely would have put something in the Constitution about separation of sex and politics; then sixteen-year-old pages in the House of Representatives could have gone into the cloakroom alone without fear of being accosted by heavy-breathing lawmakers.

On the other side of the coin, had we had a Constitutional dictum against sex and politics, we might also have been spared John and Rita Jenrette, who tried their darnedest to give heterosexuality a bad name ... and with all of us following the sordid saga on television.

10 Eddie Haskell Is Still A Jerk

I MENTIONED EARLIER that Phil Donahue and his television show have been a great source of consternation for me. Five mornings a week, Donahue gets together with a crowd of women who live in Chicago and apparently have nothing better to do, and they discuss strange things.

One morning recently, for example, his guests were two homosexual women and a baby. The two homosexual women, who said they were very much in love, had decided they wanted a baby, so one of them was artificially inseminated with the sperm of the other's brother, and the baby on the program was the result.

One of the homosexual women was black and the other was white, and I think they named the baby something like "Joy" or "Mud." I only remember that the baby didn't have a regular name like we used to give children — a name like Randy or Arlene.

I frankly don't care if a black female homosexual and a white female homosexual decide to love each other, but I do

144

have some concern for the offspring. Having been conceived in such an unconventional manner and having been given a name that would embarrass a dog, I wonder if the child will have the desire or the opportunity to do the things that are important to most children — such as playing Little League baseball, eating crayons in school, or laughing at a clown.

What bothers me about this situation in particular, and about the Donahue show in general, is where all this might lead. Television today is probably the greatest single influence on the American public. A recent study showed that the average TV in this country is on six hours and fifty-five minutes a day; that's almost forty-nine hours a week. In a ten-year period, that's almost three years of watching TV! It's not surprising, therefore, that in many cases society has become what it watches.

So my question is this: Will all these televised discussions of aberrant lifestyles eventually make such behavior completely acceptable, and will people start producing babies with home chemistry sets and giving them names that will make it difficult for them to survive when they enter the Marine Corps?

Actually, my problems with television didn't begin with Donahue. After my Aunt Jessie, who lived next door, brought home the first television I could watch on a regular basis, it took me a year to figure out that Howdy Doody was a puppet. I presumed he had once suffered from some sort of crippling disease, and that was why he walked funny. He also had a strange mouth, which I attributed to not brushing regularly. When Howdy talked, the entire bottom portion of his mouth moved like he was trying to eat a large cantaloupe. Whole.

145

Finally I noticed the strings attached to him. It was like the day I found out there is no Santa Claus and the day somebody told me they heard Lash Larue was in a porno film. It broke my heart. You know kids, though. I couldn't wait to tell everybody I knew of my discovery.

"Howdy Doody isn't real," I told one of my classmates at school.

"Yes, he is," he replied.

"No, he isn't. He's just a puppet. Somebody pulls his strings and that's what makes him walk and talk."

The kid started crying. I didn't dare tell him that Clarabelle's big red nose was probably fake, too.

Soon I discovered "Superman." I enjoyed watching "The Man of Steel," but I had some problems with him, too. In the first place, I never thought Superman's disguise as Clark Kent was all that clever. Lois Lane had to be a bigger dummy than Howdy Doody not to see right through it.

Whenever Superman decided to become Clark Kent, all he did was put on a coat and tie and a pair of glasses. That's a disguise? Superman and Clark Kent talked exactly the same, were the same height and weight, and if Lois had been any kind of reporter at all, she probably would have noticed that they had the same mole or freckle or other telltale body markings.

In retrospect, Lois Lane had no business working for *The Daily Planet*. She should have been on the obit desk in Topeka.

Something else used to bother me about the "Superman" show. Anytime "The Man of Steel" had a social misfit cornered, the crook would pull out a gun and fire six shots at Superman's chest. Of course, bullets just bounced off, because you couldn't hurt Superman.

146

Even as a kid, I knew what I would have done after that. I would have gone quietly. But not the crooks on "Superman." After watching their bullets bounce harmlessly away, they would throw their guns at him. Anybody knows you don't further rile a man whom six bullets couldn't stop by throwing your gun at him.

* * *

There were a lot of family shows on television in those early days. There was "The Donna Reed Show," for example. Donna was always so pleasant. I wonder why she never had that-time-of-the-month problems like other women?

"Father Knows Best," another great family show, was one of my favorites. Even so, I used to wonder why Robert Young never took his tie off. When he came home from a long day at the insurance office, he would keep his tie on and replace his jacket with a sweater. He did the same thing later as Marcus Welby, and remember that you never saw him without a tie on when he wound up selling Sanka. He may have been the only man in history to wear a tie more than Richard Nixon.

"Leave It to Beaver" also was a big hit. In fact, it still is. "Leave It to Beaver" reruns are on several cable stations today, and a fellow named Irwyn Applebaum has even written a book entitled, "The World According to Beaver." The book contains examples of the sort of dialogue that was featured on the show. Here's one between Wally and his friend, the ever-obnoxious Eddie Haskell.

EDDIE: "Come on, Sam, time's a-wastin'."

WALLY: "Look, Eddie, I can't go with you guys today. I've got to work out in the yard."

147

EDDIE: "Work in the yard? Aw, come off it! We got ... Oh, good morning, Mr. and Mrs. Cleaver."

JUNE: "Hello, Eddie."

WARD: "Good morning, Eddie."

EDDIE: "Well, if you've got work to do, Wallace, I don't want to interfere. I was reading an article in the paper just the other day, and it said a certain amount of responsibility around the home is good character training. Well, good-bye, Mr. and Mrs. Cleaver."

WARD: *"Good-bye,* Eddie."

EDDIE (whispering): "Can I talk to you outside, Wally?"

WALLY: "Okay, Eddie, what's up?"

EDDIE: "Come on, Moe, drop the hoe. Lumpy's out in the car and we're ready to roll."

WALLY: "I told you, Eddie. I can't. I got work to do."

EDDIE: "Come on, Isabel, you gonna let your mother and father push you around? Why don't you read them the child labor law?"

WALLY: "Hey, Eddie, isn't it about the time of year you're supposed to shed your skin?"

I take a certain amount of comfort in knowing that Eddie Haskell comes off as just as big a jerk today as he did twenty years ago. There are so few elements of life that have gone unchanged in that period.

"The Adventures of Ozzie and Harriet" was another classic of those timid times. There was Ozzie and Harriet and David and Ricky, and they lived in a big house and everybody was happy and problems were easy to solve. Television of the fifties rarely dealt with anything more intricate than a husband forgetting an anniversary or a wife burning dinner for the husband's boss.

In those days, Ozzie was always around to talk over prob-

148

lems with David and Ricky. As a matter fact, I still don't know what Ozzie did for a living; I never recall his going to work. If they did "The Adventures of Ozzie and Harriet" today, Ozzie probably would be a dope dealer.

* * *

There are a lot of things I miss about television the way it used to be. I'll take John Cameron Swayze over Peter Jennings on a big story any day, and has there ever been a better detective than Sargeant Joe Friday on "Dragnet"?

Joe Friday didn't waste a lot of time keeping Los Angeles free of crime on his program. All he wanted was the facts. Today, television cops get involved in a lot of extracurricular activities, such as fooling around with women.

(Fact: Jack Webb, who played Joe Friday, died not long ago of a heart attack. Maybe he should have taken a few days off occasionally and gone to Pismo Beach with a girlfriend.)

"Amos 'n' Andy" was a favorite at my aunt's house. George "Kingfish" Stevens was always trying to con Andrew H. Brown, and sooner or late the Kingfish would end up in court with his lawyer, Algonquin J. Calhoun, representing him:

"Yo' Honor, it's easy for the prosecutor to talk that way about my client, George Stevens. It's easy 'cause my client is a crook, Yo' Honor!"

"Amos 'n' Andy" was classic humor, but unfortunately we can't watch it on television today. It's allegedly racist.

That's just another example of how confusing the modern world has become. I can't watch "Amos 'n' Andy" because it's racist, but it's okay to watch "Sanford and Son," which is filled with racist situations and remarks.

149

Remember the time Fred had to go to the dentist? He found out that the dentist was black and insisted on having a white man work on his mouth. And don't forget his classic line, "There ain't nothin' uglier than an old white woman."

There must be some big difference in the two programs, but I swear I can't see it. Maybe it's a matter of perspective.

I remember several years ago when I was working in Chicago, the nation's most segregated city, and caught a cab home one night after work. The cab driver was black, and we began to talk.

"Where you from?" he asked.

"Atlanta."

"Thought so," he said. "I'm from Mississippi."

Here it comes, I figured. A black cabbie is about to give me a lecture on how much better life is away from the racist jackals of the South.

"I'm going back one of these day," he said instead.

I was startled. "You don't like it here?"

"People ain't the same up here," he said. "In Mississippi, they always let you know where you stand. They put up signs down there that say, 'No Niggers Allowed.' Up here, they don't put up no signs. They just let you walk into a place and then tell you you can't stay. I liked it better when I knew ahead of time where I was wanted."

I guess that's how I feel about television these days. I liked it better when I knew what was okay to laugh at and what wasn't.

It is modern television, in fact, that has helped to foster the two most offensive Southern stereotypes — the racist redneck and the belligerent country sheriff. And nothing irritates me more than to see Southerners being portrayed on television by actors or actresses who can't speak the

150

language.

Take *y'all*, for instance. Southerners never say *you all*, and even if we did, we wouldn't use it in the singular sense. The proper word, used when speaking to two or more others, is a contraction, *y'all*.

On television, however, some honey from the Bronx who has landed a part as a Southern belle inevitably says to her lover, "Why don't *you all* come ovuh heah and sit down by lil' ol' me."

I doubt that "Amos 'n' Andy" was near the embarrassment to blacks that yankees trying to portray Southerners is to Southern whites.

* * *

Television actually was responsible for my first encounter with discrimination, because it brought major league baseball into my life.

For the first time, I could *see* Mantle and Musial and Williams and Snider. I became a hardcore Dodger fan — they were still in Brooklyn then — and consequently developed a keen hatred for the Yankees.

I mentioned my love for the Dodgers one day to a cousin, who happened to be a Yankee fan. "The Dodgers!" he said, almost spitting out the words. "They're a nigger team!"

Perhaps I had overheard the older folks talking, or perhaps I had read something in the newspapers about Jackie Robinson, the first black man in major league baseball, but I never considered it when pledging my allegiance to the Dodgers. So when my older cousin made what was obviously a derogatory remark, I was hurt and confused. I pressed my cousin for more information, but all he would say was, "Niggers ain't got no business playing major league ball."

I decided to take the question to my mother. "Do niggers have any business playing major league ball?" I asked her.

"The word," she said in her sternest schoolteacher voice, "is *knee-grow*. I don't ever want to hear you say that other word in this house."

Fine, but that didn't answer the question. Frankly, I was more interested in baseball than in race relations at the time.

"I don't know anything about baseball, son," she said, "but your daddy played with Negroes in the service."

That settled it. If my father had played with Negroes, then there was no problem with Jackie Robinson playing with the Dodgers. Besides, all I wanted Robinson to do was help beat the Yankees, which is exactly what he did in the 1955 World Series.

I was so thankful for the Dodger victory that I said a prayer in church, reasoning that God, in all His infinite wisdom, certainly must be a Dodger fan, too.

* * *

Parents today are concerned that their children see too much sex and violence on television. There wasn't any sex to speak of on TV when I was a child, unless you count watching lady wrestlers tumble around with one another in those tight-fitting outfits they used to wear.

There was violence, but the victims usually deserved the thrashings they got.

Johnny Mack Brown walks into a saloon in the Five O'Clock Movie and says, "Gimme a milk." Heroes in those days didn't drink liquor, you recall.

152

"Milk?" laughs an ornery galoot standing next to JMB at the bar. "Here, tenderfoot," he continues, pushing a drink toward Johnny Mack, "try a little of this red-eye. It'll put some hair on your chest."

Johnny Mack Brown, after gulping down his milk, of course, would proceed to beat laughing boy to within an inch of his life, and the saloon would be totally destroyed in the meantime. I never thought about it much back then, but now I wonder who paid for the damages after all those saloons were destroyed.

I watched so many westerns as a kid that I'm still an expert on who rode what horse. Try me.

Gene Autry? That's a throwaway. He rode Champion. Hopalong Cassidy? A little tougher, but no problem for an expert. His horse was Topper.

How about the horses of the sidekicks? Tonto rode Scout. Frog Millhouse's horse was named Ringeye. Festus Hagan's mule on "Gunsmoke" was Ruth.

What our parents should have worried about our seeing on television was not sex and violence, but rather a way of life that was totally unrealistic — one that we would never be able to emulate. Just as viewers today are influenced by the whackos on "Donahue," we were given a model of the way a family was supposed to work when we watched early television.

Ward and June never argued on "Leave It to Beaver," and Jim and Margaret knew their roles in "Father Knows Best." Jim sat in the den with his stupid tie and sweater on, while Margaret made dinner. And none of the kids ever got into any kind of trouble that couldn't be handled in a calm family conference.

One of the most unrealistic examples which television

153

promoted was that of Roy Rogers and Dale Evans (who may have been the first feminist, now that I think about it. She kept her maiden name, and she never rode sidesaddle. Donahue would have loved her).

Roy went off everyday and fought cattle thieves, while Dale stayed home and watched over the ranch. When Roy returned, Dale cooked him something to eat, and then they'd sit around singing "Happy Trails" together. For years, "Happy Trails" was my favorite song:

> *"Happy trails to you,*
> *Until we meet again.*
> *Happy trails to you,*
> *Keep smiling until then.*
> *Happy traaaaails to youuuuuu,*
> *'Til we meeeeeet aaaaagain."*

Of course, it didn't turn out that way at all. "Happy Trails" turned into "Forty Miles of Bad Road."

I came home after a hard day's work one evening and said to my then-wife, "Rustle up some grub, woman, and call me when it's ready. Me and ol' Bullet will be out in the backyard."

"Rustle your own grub, Roy," said my wife. "I'm taking Buttermilk and heading out for a few drinks with the girls."

* * *

I'm not certain when it was that I stopped watching television on a regular basis. I think it was soon after they took "Gunsmoke" and "Have Gun Will Travel" and "Peter Gunn" and "Perry Mason" off the air and replaced them with

154

programs that gave me headaches.

I still search for the old shows — the ones that are being rerun, thank goodness. Give me Andy and Barney and Aunt Bea and Opie over "Hart to Hart" any day. And every time I flip through the channels looking for an old program and run across "Family Feud," I secretly hope that herpes can be contracted by kissing game show contestants.

I never liked "All in the Family." Everybody was always screaming at everybody else, and it made me nervous. Maude was a grumpy old bat, and that program where Tex Ritter's son John lived with those two air-brained women was horrible. Ol' Tex must still be twirling in his grave.

I don't like soap operas, because it's too hard to remember who is pregnant and by whom, and I always had a sneaking suspicion that Laverne and Shirley were gay. But then again, I don't remember ever seeing them on "Donahue."

* * *

The movies. They can get a little crazy, too. I'm all for realism, but the language they use in today's movies is atrocious. Henry Fonda and Katherine Hepburn even used dirty words in *On Golden Pond*. And if they ever made *Gone With the Wind* over again, I can't even imagine how Rhett would tell Scarlett to take a hike this time — "Frankly, my dear, I don't ...."

When it comes to sex, movies are like everything else today — overloaded. I enjoyed sex in movies more when you *thought* they were going to do it, but you were never quite sure.

In those days, when it became apparent that a couple had

155

more on their minds than playing a few hands of canasta, the leading man and lady would embrace while doing-it music (violins and harps) played in the background. Then before they removed the first stitch of clothes, the camera faded off.

As a matter of fact, whenever you heard doing-it music in a movie, you knew it was safe to leave your seat and go buy a package of Milk Duds, because absolutely nothing was going to happen that you hadn't seen before. Today if you leave your seat for even a couple of minutes, you're liable to miss three gang rapes, two oral sex scenes, and enough skin to re-upholster an entire Greyhound bus.

It doesn't have to be that way, of course. Great movies still can be made without having a nudist colony as the setting. Take *Tender Mercies*, for example; Robert Duvall won an Academy Award for his performance and never took off more than his shirt.

What we need is more movies like *The Natural* and *Patton*, my all-time favorite movie. George C. Scott was even better than his cousin Randolph. I also enjoy action movies where the villains gets theirs in the end — movies like *Walking Tall*, where Joe Don Baker took a stick and destroyed an entire Tennessee roadhouse and everybody inside it.

Unfortunately, I doubt that movies ever will be the same as they used to be. Back then we went for diversion and relaxation and Milk Duds, not for some deep, sensitive message; not to see people butchered with chain saws; not to see things you used to see only in the magazines your older brother brought home from the Navy.

I give credit to the brilliant Chicago columnist Mike Royko for putting today's movies in their proper perspective. Royko sensed that when John Wayne died, the movie

156

industry changed forevermore.

In his tribute to the Duke, Royko cited the way he handled Dirty Ned Pepper in *True Grit,* and he wondered how John Travolta would have dealt with Dirty Ned in the same situation.

"He probably would have asked him to dance," wrote Royko.

11 Who Does My Butt Belong To Now?

Sin, like practically every other element of life, isn't as simple as it used to be. And retribution, which always seemed to involve my rear end in one way or another, isn't as firm or as fast as it once was.

Of course, there are many more opportunities to sin today than there were twenty years ago. Combine that with the obvious erosion of discipline and respect for authority, and what you have is a lot of young people running around having loads of fun doing things it never occurred to the youth of twenty years ago to do.

We've already discussed sex. With the pill for safety and the *Penthouse* Forum for directions, who knows what's going on in the back seats of Toyotas these days? Whatever it is, I'm certain that the participants are much more cramped than they would have been had the 1957 Chevy lived on into the eighties.

Peeping Tomism, which was popular with my generation, also has lost its way in the modern world. We used to slip

158

around and snoop in windows to see if we could catch girls in their underclothing. Kids today get their equivalent kicks by using computers to invade the privacy of large corporations. I suppose they see enough skin on television and in the newspaper ads for movies; they don't have to waste their time crouching outside of windows. But if I had to pick, I still would rather watch Kathy Sue Loudermilk do her famous eight-o'clock-every-Wednesday-evening striptease from the tree outside her bedroom than to gaze at the financial records of AT&T in my computer.

The sin of gluttony has even changed since I was growing up. We used to steal watermelons and then gorge ourselves. I was even known to gnaw on the rinds when I was feeling especially gluttonous. Kids today pig-out on Slurpies and Twinkies and Little Debbie Snack Cakes, and they can get pizza delivered to their doorsteps. And not long ago I was at Baskin-Robbins behind a kid who was having trouble deciding which of the thirty-one flavors he wanted, so he finally said, "I'll just have a scoop of each." When I left, he had eaten down through the Almond Toffee and was working on the Fudge Swirl and washing it all down with Tab.

Frankly, I'm glad that I'm not twenty years younger and confronted with all the temptations that the nation's youth face today. I'm glad, for example, that I never had to deal with the issue of drugs.

There certainly were no drugs in my high school, and a real druggie when I was in college was someone who took No-Doz. We knew from seeing Sal Mineo in *The Gene Krupa Story* that a thing called marijuana existed, but we had never seen any. We figured that only kids in New York City smoked it, and that was why they all looked so greasy and undernourished.

159

The only thing we took to alter our mental state was beer or maybe bourbon mixed with Coke. Even that was only an occasional indulgence, because beginning drinkers (as most of us were) spent a lot of time embracing the stone pony. That means we spent a lot of time throwing up into a commode, and that definitely wasn't cool.

Had drugs been available in my school days, there would have been some to try them, no doubt. Norris Brantley, for instance. He would try anything.

Norris had a big date one evening, but his parents had made him spend the afternoon painting the garage. When Norris finished, he was covered in paint and had only an hour to make himself presentable for his date. He showered and scrubbed, but he couldn't get the paint off his arms and legs.

Norris had heard that gasoline was a marvelous paint remover, so he siphoned several buckets full out of his mother's car and filled the tub. Then he sat soaking in the gasoline, waiting for it to remove the paint.

Meanwhile, Norris's mother was busy hostessing a bridge party.

"Do you smell gas fumes, Marjorie?" one of the ladies said to Mrs. Brantley.

Soon all the ladies smelled the fumes, and Mrs. Brantley began searching through the house to find the source. The closer she got to Norris's bathroom, the stronger the scent became.

She finally looked in the bathroom and found Norris sprawled out in the tub. He had passed out from breathing the gasoline fumes. Moving quickly, Mrs. Brantley pulled Norris out of the tub and, using a fireman's carry, hauled him out of the bathroom, through the den where the bridge

160

ladies were, and out into the yard. After a few minutes, Norris revived.

Mrs. Brantley then went back inside and attempted to revive two of the bridge ladies, who had fainted at the sight of Mrs. Brantley carrying ol' naked Norris through the den.

That was the last time Norris ever tried to take a gasoline bath, but later on he tried something even more daring. He actually ate the "mystery meat" they served us in the high school cafeteria on Wednesdays, which was worse than the Friday meatloaf that had been forced upon us back at Moreland elementary.

Previously, no student had been brave enough to attempt the Wednesday mystery meat. It defied description and categorization. It was a dark, hideous-looking substance which the cooks tried to hide by covering it with gravy. Whenever a student would ask, "What is this?", the cooks would simply look at each other and smile knowingly. They would never answer the question.

Norris, who had eaten an entire package of crayons in third-grade art class on a dare, became so intrigued by the mystery meat that he actually cut a piece with his knife and fork, which required a considerable struggle, and ate it.

"What does it taste like?" somebody asked Norris.

"Sort of like a blue crayon," he answered.

We never did learn the identity of the mystery meat, but Norris later reported that he took a piece home and tried to feed it to his dog. The dog ran and hid under the bed and wouldn't come out until Norris buried the substance in the yard.

Norris would drink anything, too. We were on a camping trip when one of the kids from out in the country produced a pint of his father's white liquor, known to some as "moonshine."

"Let me have a chug of that," Norris said to the kid with the pint.

"You need to strain it first," said the kid. "It's got some leaves and dead bugs in it."

That was no problem for Norris. He took off his T-shirt and strained the pint through it. Then he took a deep pull out of the jar.

When Norris got his breath back, he said, "It ain't much to taste, but next time I got to paint the garage, I sure could use a couple of gallons."

* * *

Most of us were quite satisfied with drinking beer. The only problem was obtaining it. Unless your parents went out of town and left some in the refrigerator, or you had an older brother who would buy it for you, or you had an understanding uncle who would bring you out a case from the Moose Club, you normally had to resort to bribing curb boys.

I drank my first beer when I was six. I found a half-full can on the coffee table one morning after my parents had entertained the evening before. They were still in bed, so I picked up the can and drank what was left in it. Having never tasted cold beer, I wasn't bothered in the least that this was warm. As a matter of fact, I quite enjoyed it, and afterwards I began singing "She'll Be Coming Around the Mountain," my favorite song when I was six. Then I took myself a long nap.

I didn't try another beer until I was fourteen. Nathanial, one of the curb waiters at Steve Smith's truckstop, brought

162

Danny Thompson and me three tall-boy Carling Black Labels out to the back of the truckstop for the price of the beer plus a dollar for his risk and trouble.

I drank my Carling Black Labels faster than Danny did, so I threw up first. We walked home — both of us quite ill.

It was a warm night. We had no air conditioning at my house, but I was still sober enough to remember how cool the inside of a refrigerator feels on a hot summer night in Georgia. So I sat down next to the refrigerator, opened the door, and stuck my head inside on one of the racks.

Then, just as I had done eight years earlier, I took a little nap. It was in that position, sleeping with my head stuck between lettuce and banana pudding in the refrigerator, that my mother found me a couple of hours later.

"Why are you sleeping in the refrigerator?" she asked.

"I was going to get myself some leftover banana pudding," I answered, "but it was so nice and cool in here that I decided to take a nap."

I always underestimated my mother's ability to tell when I was lying.

"Let me smell your breath," she said. "I think you've been drinking."

I was dead. I let her smell my breath.

"How much did you have?" she asked.

"Two cans of beer that I remember," I answered. "I'm a little hazy on the third one."

"Did it make you sick?"

"As a dog."

"Where did you get it?"

"Curb waiter at Steve's."

My mother put me to bed, and the next morning, as I lay hovering between life and death, she brought me aspirin. I expected her to give me a long lecture about drinking, but instead all she said was, "I hope you've learned a lesson."

And I had. I learned never to drink Carling Black Label beer on a warm evening and never to stick my head in a refrigerator unless I'm wide awake.

* * *

The more I think about it, the more I'm convinced that most of us wouldn't have gotten involved with drugs even if they had been available. Our parents certainly did not condone drinking, but at least there had been beer when they were young, and most of them knew the appeal it held for adolescents.

But not drugs. They would have been outraged, and they would have cracked down hard on us. And I don't think we would have rebelled against them, either, because their disciplinary measures were fast and firm in those days.

These were not people to be trifled with. They had learned from the harsh parenting they had received, and they would stop at nothing to be sure that we understood they were in complete control.

My own dear mother had a strict rule that I was not allowed, under any circumstances, to ride on any mechanized vehicle that had less than four wheels. What she had in mind specifically was Dudley Stamps's motor scooter.

When Dudley was fourteen, his parents bought him a motor scooter. My mode of transportation at the time still required a great deal of pedaling. Dudley would ride into my yard on his scooter and invite me to go for a spin.

"You aren't going to get on any motor scooter," my mother would insist. "You could fall off and break your

164

neck."

I knew I wasn't going to fall off and break my neck, but I couldn't convince my mother of that. When I was younger, she had been the same way about my running with a sharp stick in my hand.

"Put that stick down, young man!" she would scream at me. "You might fall and put out your eye."

For years, I have been following the papers trying to find just one instance of a child running with a sharp stick in his hand and falling and putting out an eye. I have yet to come across one, but I suppose that's the result of the constant vigil of mothers guarding against running and carrying sharp sticks simultaneously.

I rarely disobeyed my mother, but one day Dudley came by on his scooter and my mother wasn't home.

"We'll just be gone a few minutes," Dudley said. "She'll never know you went for a ride."

The thrill of riding on the scooter caused me to lose all track of time. When I returned home three hours later, my mother went into hysterics. She sentenced me to no television for a month, forbade me ever to be in the company of Dudley Stamps again until I had children of my own, and fed me liver twice a week for three months. I considered myself lucky that parents didn't have the right to give the death penalty in cases of such extreme disobedience.

I get the impression that parents of children today, in most instances, do not rule their disobedient young with the strong hand of discipline and authority that once was used.

Some parents think nothing today of allowing their fourteen-year-olds to hang out at rock concerts. Even if it weren't for all the known evils (see earlier reference to Elton John concert), attendance at such events obviously is having a

165

detrimental effect on the hearing of today's youth. Nobody can listen to that much sound without suffering some degree of hearing impairment. Perhaps many of our children already have suffered severe hearing loss, which is why they think the music at rock concerts is appealing.

The schools aren't nearly as strict as they once were, either. If a teacher spanks a child today, she may have a lawsuit on her hands. But that's another reason I don't think many members of my generation would have gotten involved with drugs and dyed their hair orange and exhibited all the rebellious, independent behavior of seventies and eighties youth. If our parents hadn't stopped us from such, the folks at school would have had a field day with our hindparts.

Not long ago I ran into one of my former teachers.

"It was never the same after your class (Class of '64)," he said. "You were the last class that took it as we dished it out. I've missed you."

Certainly the children changed, but I wonder if the teachers didn't, too. I wonder if their growing fears of lawsuits and even their fears of some of the students didn't cause them to lose their grip.

My old high school principal, O.P. Evans, is dead now. Maybe what killed him was living long enough to see discipline erode in the public school system.

Mr. Evans always began each student assembly by reading from his worn Bible, which was held together by a few rubberbands and the grace of the book's main character. I can hear him now, booming out from the Word:

"'When I was a child, I spoke as a child ... but when I became a man, I put away childish things.'"

That was Mr. Evans's way of saying that any student

166

caught chewing gum in study hall would be beaten within an inch of his or her life. O.P. had rules and enforced them.

— No gum chewing anytime or anywhere.

— A student caught smoking faced certain suspension. This included smoking on weekends and before and after school. O.P. Evans held that when a student entered his high school, the student belonged to him until graduation.

— No fooling around between male and female students. When walking down the halls with a member of the opposite sex, for instance, a student was to maintain at least twelve inches of space between himself and herself. Those who violated this rule were taken to Mr. Harris's health class, where he lectured about pregnancy, venereal disease, and saving yourself for your life's partner.

— Any student missing time from school must bring a detailed excuse written and signed by his parents. Norris Brantley once was out of school for several days at the same time his parents were conveniently out of town. Norris attempted to write his own excuse. It said, "Please excuse Norris from class. He was real sick Oct. 29, 30, 31, and 32." As punishment, they made him eat two helpings of mystery meat for every day he was out of school.

Mr. Evans's wife, Mrs. Evans to us, was head librarian. She had rules, too:

— No reading a library book before you washed your hands. Any library book turned in with a smudge on any page would bring punishment for the smudger. I always read library books wearing the rubber gloves my mother used for washing dishes.

— No sound whatsoever in the library. This included throat-clearing, sneezing, coughing, and the sound a chair makes when it's pulled out from under a table for the purpose of sitting.

— Boys were required to remove watches and girls were required to remove any rings or bracelets while sitting at a library table, in order that the tables not be scratched.

There were no scratches on the tables in the Newnan High Library, the place was quieter than a cemetery at midnight, and there were no smudges on the books. Students took little advantage of what the library had to offer, however; it's difficult to read *Les Miserables,* for instance, when you feel like somebody is behind you holding a .45 to your head. *Go ahead, punk. Smudge that book and make my day.*

The superintendent of schools was Homer Drake. Mr. Drake wasn't a bad sort, but he had a habit of appearing unannounced in class to check on his teachers. For that reason, the teachers were terribly nervous all the time. They felt the heat of the same .45, I suppose. Consequently, very little of what went on in a Newnan High School class was frivolous. You couldn't even relax and have a few laughs in shop, lest Mr. Drake walk in and catch somebody actually enjoying themselves. The pursuit of knowledge was serious business to Homer Drake.

For added effect, Mr. Drake occasionally dropped into study hall and walked through the rows of desks pulling on boys' ears. Not only is it impossible to work out algebraic equations while the school superintendent is pulling on your ear, but it's also quite painful. One day I noticed that Mr. Drake had very large ears. I reasoned that somebody had pulled on his ears when he was a young man and this was his way of showing us that he was just one of the guys. I would have preferred that he went around goosing us in the belly instead of pulling on our ears.

My high school had traditional instructors, too. There

168

was Mr. Hearn, the shop teacher, for example.

"Boys," he would begin his classes every year, "the most important thing to remember while working with an electric saw is safety." With that remark, he would hold up his right hand, which was missing its two middle fingers.

We had a wonderful American history teacher named Miss McGruder. She resembled a frog. In fact, her homeroom was called "The Pond." One day she called on Harley Doakes to tell her what he had read the night before in the assignment concerning President James K. Polk.

Harley stammered for an answer.

"You don't know anything about President Polk, Harley?" she pressed.

Harley searched his mind, a brief endeavor, and finally answered, "Was he the one who invented polk and beans?"

Miss McGruder sent a note to Harley's parents, informing them of how he had answered her question.

"I'm proud of you, son," Harley's dad said to him at supper after he read the note. "I certainly didn't know where polk and beans came from."

Miss Garland taught geometry. She was very old and about half-blind. All of her students made high grades in geometry, because if a student could make a few straight lines on the blackboard with a piece of chalk, Miss Garland couldn't see well enough to know whether or not he had solved the problem correctly. She would simply squint at the board for a few seconds and say, "Oh, child, you do such grand work."

Ronnie Jenkins once drew a picture of some unidentifiable four-legged creature on the board. Miss Garland thought he had dissected an angle. She gave Ronnie an A, even though he thought an hypotenuse was a large animal he saw once at the Grant Park Zoo in Atlanta.

The teacher who ran study hall was Mrs. Carpenter, an ex-WAC sergeant. She allowed no foolishness, either. Students were to keep their eyes forward and on their books at all times ... or give her twenty-five quick push-ups.

In the stillness and silence of Mrs. Carpenter's study hall one afternoon, my eyes facing my book, I began to hum. I don't remember why; I just began to hum. The person behind me picked it up and started to hum, too. Soon, seventy-five of us were humming, our eyes still on our books and our mouths closed.

"Who's doing that humming?" shouted Mrs. Carpenter. We continued to hum.

"Stop that humming right now, or I'll send you all to Mr. Evans's office," she warned.

When we still wouldn't quit humming, she marched all seventy-five of us toward the principal's office.

"I had a good home, but I left, right, left, right....," she called out as we maneuvered down the hallway.

When Mr. Evans could not convince anyone to admit to malicious humming, he decided to punish us by administering an across-the-board, one-letter cut in citizenship grades on our next report cards. He also assigned us to memorize the Beatitudes out of the Book of Matthew. (The meek shall inherit the earth, and woe be unto the fool who hums in study hall.)

Students in future times would burn buildings, smoke dope in the hallways, pull knives on teachers, have frequent sexual encounters with one another, and listen to strange music sung by strange people with pink hair and safety pins stuck through their earlobes. We just hummed.

170

WHO DOES MY BUTT BELONG TO NOW?

* * *

Baby Boomers like myself went off to college in droves. Never before had a larger percentage of a generation pursued higher education. More than being what *we* wanted, it was what our parents wanted, what they had saved and scrimped for, what they had dreamed about.

We want you to have it better than we did, they said time and again, and one way we were going to have it better was to be educated. My mother, a teacher, rarely spent money on herself. She watched every penny that came in and went out of the house, and she hoarded many of them for my college.

There were few people in my hometown who had been to college. Among some of the old folks, there was even the classic resentment for and suspicion of someone who had gone, or was going, to college.

I walked into Cureton and Cole's one day, and some of the old men were seated around the stove.

"Heard you goin' off to college," said one.

"University of Georgia," I answered proudly.

"Don't you get too big for your britches and forget where you came from," I was instructed.

"I won't."

"I tell you something, when I come along, there wadn't no way you could go to college. Hell, my daddy jerked my tail out of school when I was twelve years old to help him bring in the crop. I got an education, but it wadn't from no college. I got it from behind a mule."

Somehow, I felt like a traitor. These were my people, my roots.

"I've seen a lot of 'em go off to college and get a lot of book sense, but then they still ain't got no common sense.

171

Couldn't plow a straight row if their life depended on it."

"Most of 'em go off to college in the first place 'cause they don't want to do a honest day's work."

"Hey, college boy, what you going to study for? You goan be one of them smart-ass lawyers like they got up in the city?"

I said I wasn't certain what I was going to study.

"Why don't you study to be a schoolteacher like you' mama?" somebody asked.

I said school teaching didn't appeal to me. Besides, there wasn't much money in it, I added.

"Money? That's all they think about today is money, especially them damn lawyers."

"Hey, you know the difference between a dead lawyer in the highway and a dead possum in the highway?"

"Naw."

"Dead lawyer ain't got no skid marks in front of him."

I said I'd better be leaving, but before I could go, Harvey (Dynamite) Garfield, Frankie's older brother, walked in.

"Hey, Dynamite," somebody said, "what do you think of college-boy here going off to get an education?"

"Well, it's just like I told that smart sonofabitch foreman of mine at the mill," Dynamite began. "I told him I wanted to get off the third shift and get me one of them day jobs in the office. He said I needed an education for that. I told him I didn't have no edugoddamncation, but I could whip his ass with one hand. He's goan see what he can do about my promotion."

They were still hooting as I walked out the door. I had learned a lot through the years, sitting and listening around the stove. But at that moment, I knew I would never be as welcome again. There was no place for a college boy in the

172

Order of the Stove. At that moment, I also knew my hometown never would be the same again. I was leaving it, and it would stay the same, but I would broaden.

I wondered if I would miss it. I wondered how often I would come back and, when I did, how I would be accepted — as one to be respected because he had seen the lamp of knowledge, or one to be ostracized because he felt that he wasn't good enough, that he needed to rise above his roots?

I decided two things: (1) No matter how much they had laughed and hooted, no matter what anybody thought, getting an edugoddamncation was important, especially for somebody who couldn't mug his foreman; and (2) I decided I would not go to law school.

* * *

Stories and legends abounded concerning what a young man could expect once he entered the University of Georgia, the nation's oldest state chartered university, which was also known — to those back in the hinterlands high schools — as The Promised Land.

I arrived on the Athens campus in September, 1964, one month before my eighteenth birthday, and was assigned a corner room in Reed Hall. My roommate, who had been selected without consulting me, was a French major who smoked Pall Mall cigarettes. In the evenings, he would sit and smoke and listen to Edith Piaff records in the haze of light coming from a blue bulb in his desk lamp.

We lasted a month together. I finally managed to get transferred to a new room and acquired a new roommate — George Cobb, Jr., from Greenville, South Carolina, whose father built golf courses. George and I got along famously.

173

After two or three weeks together, we decided to redecorate our room. The university had furnished our tiny cubicle with one bunk bed, two desks, and a couple of hard-back chairs. A monk would have been uncomfortable in that stark environment.

George and I rented a truck and went to a used furniture store in Athens. For fifty dollars, we purchased a used sofa, lounge chair, and ottoman. Fellow freshmen came from dorms all over the campus to view our newly refurbished room.

The University of Georgia had all sorts of rules concerning housing in 1964. Among them were:

— No alcohol inside dormitories.

— No females inside dormitories.

— No used sofas, lounge chairs, nor ottomans inside dormitories.

We had not been apprised of the third rule when we decided to redecorate, so it was somewhat of a surprise when the dean of housing paid George and me a visit one evening.

"What is all this?" the dean, a stern man, asked.

"What is all what, sir?" asked George.

"This ragged furniture," said the dean. "Where did it come from?"

"Farmer's Furniture, sir," George answered. "We think it gives the place a homey look."

"I want it out of here in the morning," the dean continued.

"Sir," said George, a business major, "this furniture represents an investment of fifty dollars on the part of my roommate and I. We also feel it is conducive to improving our study habits, because now that our room is more comfort-

174

able, we are more anxious to remain here and do our work. Could you give us some reason why we can't have furniture in our room?"

"I want it out of here by morning, or I'll kick both your butts out of school," the dean said.

Farmer's Furniture gave us only thirty dollars for the used furniture we had bought there five days earlier for fifty. We had, however, learned two new facts:

Fact one: Used furniture depreciates in value at a very fast rate.

Fact two: My butt, which once belonged to my parents and to O.P. Evans, now was under the control of the dean of housing at the University of Georgia.

But despite that unpleasant run-in with university officialdom, George and I were finding out that most of the legends we had heard concerning campus life in Athens were, indeed, true.

The beer flowed freely at Georgia. There was Allen's and Uppy's and Sarge's Place and Harry's and the Black Horse Inn, formerly the legendary Old South, located just across the street from the campus and just above the bus station. The story was still passed around about the student who spent an afternoon at Old South, then walked outside and got into his sports car that was parked in front of the bar.

As he drove to the first stoplight, his brakes failed and he drove squarely into the bus station, his car coming to rest at the ticket counter. Amidst the screams and the shattered glass, he leaned out of his car and said to the man behind the ticket counter, "Roundtrip to Savannah, please."

The best place to buy packaged beer in Athens was at Bubber's Bait Shop, which over the years had become an institution of sorts. Bubber, a gentle man, knew all his student customers by name and welcomed them with the same greeting: "Whaddahyouhave?"

"Six-pack of Blue Ribbon, Bubber."

"Bottles or cans?"

"Cans."

"Short or tall?"

"Tall."

"How 'bout a little Red Hurricane Wine to go with that?"

"I don't need any wine, Bubber."

"Ain't but ninety-seven cents a bottle."

"Next time, Bubber."

"That Red Hurricane Wine'll put hair on your chest."

"How much for the beer, Bubber?"

"Two-seventy-five with tax."

"Thanks, Bubber."

"Come again."

Bubber likely became quite wealthy selling beer at the Bait Shop, but he always was the same old Bubber. He was a very trustworthy individual, who also served as an occasional lending agency for financially-down-and-out students. Something else nice about Bubber — whenever a student was kicked out of school and stopped to say good-bye and buy a six-pack for the long ride home, Bubber often would drop a bottle of Red Hurricane wine in their sack for free.

"You going to need that," Bubber would say. "You got a lot of explaining to do."

Allen's was a legendary beer and hamburger joint where, the rumor went, a young man could drink all the draft beer he pleased at twenty-five cents a glass, regardless of whether or not he had sufficient proof that he was twenty-one, the legal drinking age in Georgia at the time.

My roommate George and I tested the rumor one fine autumn evening during our freshman year. Three dollars worth of draft beer each later, we were in a rather festive mood, and George began to do his impression of the sound a mule makes. It was pure genius. First, George would make a whistling sound, and then he would do a rather throaty and low "Haaaaw!" It went something like, "Hrrrrrrt! Haaaaaw!"

I was terribly impressed.

"You try it," said George.

"Hrrt! Haaaaw!" I brayed.

"More whistle," said George.

"Hrrrrrt! Haaaaaw!" I continued.

"Perfect," said George.

After the manager of Allen's asked us to leave, George decided it would be great sport to go over in front of Farm-House, a fraternity for agricultural students, and make mule sounds.

"Hrrrrrrt! Haaaaaaw!" went George out front of Farm-House.

"Hrrrrrrt! Haaaaaaw!" I followed.

After that, we did chickens and goats and cows and ducks, and George had just broken into his rooster (not as good as his mule but still quite effective) when the smiling campus policeman got out of his car and ordered our drunken butts, as he put it, into the back seat.

He drove us to our dorm room and sent us inside, but not before taking our student I.D.'s and informing us that we would hear from the Dean of Men's office the very next morning, which we most certainly did.

Dean William Tate was a campus institution at Georgia and a gentle person until riled. We had first seen Dean Tate

177

during orientation week, when freshmen men were summoned to his annual briefing about what was considered acceptable and unacceptable behavior of students.

The dean had also told his favorite joke, the one he'd been telling freshmen students for years. It involved Robert Toombs, a Georgia student in the middle nineteenth century who later ran for governor of the state. When the Civil War broke out, Toombs joined the Confederate Army and solicited troops in front of the courthouse in Marietta, Georgia, just outside Atlanta.

"I'll tell you, men, we can whoop them yankees with cornstalks," Toombs had said to his listeners in Marietta.

After the war, Toombs came back to that same courthouse for a campaign speech. In the middle of his many promises to his audience, a man spoke up.

"Mr. Toombs," he said, "I stood right here before the war and heard you ask us to jine up with the Confederate Army. I jined and my brother jined. I got shot in the Battle of Chickamaugua and my brother got shot at Antietam. You told us then we could whoop the yankees with cornstalks. I believed you then, and I paid for it. So why should I believe you now?"

Toombs paused for a few moments and then replied, "Well, we could have whooped the yankees with cornstalks, but the sons of bitches wouldn't fight that way."

We had laughed at his story then, but we didn't crack a smile when we wound up in his office. "What in the hell did you two boys think you were doing last night?" he asked me and George.

"Just kidding around, sir," answered George.

"You boys got a strange sense of humor," said Dean Tate. "I take it you had been drinking to excess."

178

"We just had a couple of beers, sir," said George.

"Takes more than a couple of beers to make a man stand outside at two o'clock in the morning cock-a-doodle-dooing. You boys were drunk, weren't you?"

We admitted it.

"I ought to kick both your butts out of school," Dean Tate said.

There was a pause as he stared at us over his glasses. I'm certain George was thinking the same thing I was: How do you explain to your parents that you have been kicked out of school for drunken cock-a-doodle-dooing?

Finally, the dean spoke again. "But I'm going to give you boys one more chance. I'm also going to make you a promise: If I see you two roosters in here one more time, you will be only a memory around this institution. Is that clear?"

It was clear.

"We appreciate your faith in us, sir," said George.

We immediately went to Allen's to celebrate our good fortune of being able to remain in school. George lifted his first glass of beer to mine.

"To Dean Tate," he said.

"A fair man," I answered.

"To FarmHouse fraternity," said George.

"Cock-a-doodle-doo," I answered him.

"To our butts," toasted George.

"To our butts," I toasted back.

I suppose what has happened to discipline and authority these days is that most everybody has a lot more control over his or her own butt than they used to. But I'm not so certain that's all for the better.

There have been many times, even recently, when I wished somebody would take charge of mine again, if for no other reason than to render the much-needed service of pointing out to me when I was about to put it on exhibition.

12 Women Don't Wear Jocks

THE CURRENT PERIOD in which we're living is probably the worst time in history to be a man. Just my luck. We had it absolutely made for thousands of years. Cave men did a little hunting now and then, but that was about it, and they ruled their women and their roosts with clubs. If the wife, or whatever cave men called their mates in those days, got a little out of hand, a gentle tap on the head did wonders in readjusting her attitude.

Later, when men became more civilized and learned how much fun it was to fight wars, they all got together on horseback and went and sacked other countries. They raped and pillaged and generally had high times.

Throughout most of history, men stuck together and did manly things and talked about manly things. In an attempt to sustain their elite and separate status over women, they formed male-only clubs, such as the Jaycees. The Supreme Court ruled recently that the Jaycees no longer can exclude women from their membership; that's an indication of how much slippage there has been in the area of male domination.

Some men today feel as though they should apologize for their fathers' attitudes toward women, and many of us have been made to feel woefully inadequate in the face of the rising force of feminism, which seems dedicated to telling men everything that is unacceptable about us.

The litany of our alleged failures is long.

Women are quick to inform us that we are lousy in bed and that we don't know how to satisfy them sexually. There is a feminist joke which says it all. A feminist asks a man, "What does a woman say when she has been totally and completely and incredibly satisfied sexually?"

The man walks into her little trap and answers politely, so he won't spoil her joke, "I don't know."

"I didn't think you would," returns the feminist, and once again the man is made to feel like a fool.

Think of all the other complaints today's women have with men: We work too hard, we're too ambitious, we drink too much, we aren't sensitive enough, and we care more about watching a stupid ball game on television than we do about spending "quality time" (a new eighties term) with them. We sexually harass women in the work environment (formerly known as the "office"), we choose which woman is to be promoted within the firm based on breast size rather than professional ability (That made sense for several hundred years. It's difficult to change overnight), and we refuse to pay women salaries equal to those men get for doing the same job — which isn't fair, of course, but it also isn't fair that men have to shave before they go to work every day, and women don't.

Not only have the Jaycees lost their ability to exclude

182

women, but it is almost impossible to keep women out of any location formerly reserved for men only. (Location, nothing! Women are even wearing men's underwear these days, and one smart-aleck feminist was quoted as saying, "It's only fair. Men have been trying to get in ours for years," which is a really blatant sexist remark if you think about it. I'm glad I don't have to resort to such a low grade of humor to get my points across.)

I am a former sportswriter. When I was covering sports, all press box tickets included the warning, "No women allowed in press box."

This wasn't because sportswriters didn't want women around when they were busy covering ball games; it was because the people who ran the press boxes knew that sportswriters in general are people who never let work get in the way of a good time. Were women not excluded from the press boxes, there wouldn't be room for everybody to sit down, what with all the writers and the cocktail waitresses they had met the night before.

Excluding women from the press box is against all sorts of laws these days, however, so even if a male writer did bring a cocktail waitress to the game with him, she probably would have to stand, because all the extra seats have been taken up by female sportswriters.

I must make another confession here. I'm certain there are many females eminently qualified to cover and report on sporting events, but I still would rather read a male's report, because I am not convinced, and never will be convinced, that women fully understand the subtleties and nuances of certain athletic events.

Okay, so allow women to cover tennis matches. Tennis is a very simple game. The person who hits the last winning shot wins the match. Professional tennis players like John McEnroe and Chris Evert are always complaining that the press is more interested in their private lives than in their tennis. That's because tennis, although loads of fun to play (I'm an incurable participant in the sport, myself. I have no talent for the game, but playing all afternoon certainly makes the evening beer taste better), is not that interesting to read about. I had much rather know why Chris dumped John than why she won't change her tactics and play serve-and-volley against Martina Navratilova. I already know why she won't come to the net against Martina: She's afraid that big ol' girl will knock her head off with a topspin forehand.

So it's okay with me if women cover tennis, and they can cover golf, too. If tennis is boring to read about, golf is a sleeping pill. Women can also report on other sports that encourage dozing, such as marathon races, bowling, swimming, gymnastics, ice skating, track, field, and soccer. In fact, women can even cover pro basketball and it won't bother me, because pro basketball is simple, too. The team with the biggest black man usually wins ... unless it happens to be the Boston Celtics, who have Larry Bird (the only white man in the last twenty years who doesn't suffer from the dreaded "white man's disease," which causes slowness afoot and the inability to jump very high).

What I strongly object to is women covering football and baseball, because they've never played either sport. Men are born with the innate ability to understand the blitz in football and the hit-and-run in baseball. Women may learn the basics of these sports, but I daresay few really watch anything more than how cute the football players' butts look in those tight pants, or how baseball players spend an inordinate amount of time scratching their privates and adjusting

184

certain necessary athletic equipment that's worn under the uniform.

In fact, that may be the crux of the problem: Women cannot achieve credibility as sports reporters with men because we know they've never worn a jock strap. And if they have, I don't want to read an inside look at the problems of the Atlanta Braves' pitching staff written by some woman who obviously has problems of her own.

If women winning their way into press boxes wasn't enough (and it wasn't), women later insisted that they also be allowed to go into the locker rooms in order to hear the pearls of wisdom that players dispatch to the press following the games. I speak from authority here, because for many years it was my job to go into dressing rooms and to be the recipient of these pearls.

Players say things like: "Well, you know, I, you know, caught the, you know, ball, and then, you know, I ran, you know, just as fast, you know, as I, you know, could, and I, you know, would like to, you know, give, you know, God the credit, you know, for, you know, making me, you know, a, you know, rich superstar."

While the players are, you know, treating the press to these marvelous exhibitions of their ability to express themselves, you know, they normally are quite naked. I'm not certain what it is about ball players, but they like to sit around naked a lot, dangling their participles at whomever happens by to speak with them.

When women first attempted to enter players' locker rooms, authorities tried to block them. But a court order here and a court order there, and suddenly post-game dressing rooms, with the players sitting in front of their lockers and all sorts of women running around with notepads, looked like a Saturday afternoon flea market.

When women no longer could be kept out of dressing rooms, most players were forced to put on bathrobes. I have noticed over the past few years that athletes do not seem nearly as dedicated and don't hustle and give their all as much as they once did. This could be due to the fact that they no longer can look forward to sitting around naked after games.

"I mean, you know, before these, you know, broads started, you know, coming in here, you know, asking a lot of, you know, questions, and looking, you know, at us like we were, you know, just big hunks of, you know, meat, we could, you know, relax after the, you know, game. Man, we could, you know, sit here without no, you know, clothes on, and sort of, you know, mellow out and, you know, think about next year's, you know, contract. You know what I mean?"

I know exactly what they mean. Men enjoy and relish the companionship of other men. They simply need to be off with other men occasionally, with no women around, so they can feel comfortable expressing their thoughts and frustrations and can pass gas without having to apologize for it. (Incidentally, that's how the Jaycees originally grew to be such a large and popular organization. I think women are going to be terribly disappointed when they join the Jaycees and find out that it was nothing more than a bunch of guys getting together once a week to have some lunch and talk about raising money for charities and passing gas in peace.)

Men learn some of the most important lessons in life from hanging around with other men. Let's take baseball, for instance. Baseball is a man's game. Women get more involved with football because it's played only once a week and there's a lot of pageantry involved, but women think

186

baseball is dull.

"Why doesn't somebody *do* something?" they ask when the tension has reached the cutting edge in a baseball game. Meanwhile, the manager in the dugout is flashing signals to the third-base coach, who relays them to the batter; the catcher is trying to keep the runner on second base from stealing his signal to the pitcher; and the pitcher is signaling a pick-off attempt to the shortstop. And she asks why doesn't somebody do something.

In addition to that, the hit-and-run is completely lost on most women, and no woman on earth, even an exceptionally smart one, can comprehend the infield fly rule and why baseball simply wouldn't work very well without it.

I played baseball from the time I was five until I was eighteen, and I learned all sorts of manly things that I probably couldn't have learned anywhere else. I learned to cuss, for instance.

There are different curse words for different baseball situations. Let's say you've just led off the game at the plate and the pitcher has struck you out. When you return, bat in hand, to the dugout, the other players always inquire, "What's he got?", meaning, Is the pitcher talented?

Baseball, a *macho* sport, is very competitive by nature. No man who has just struck out to start a game is about to give the pitcher any credit, so he always answers the above question by declaring, "The sonofabitch ain't got a thing."

"Come on!" the other players then beseech the second batter, "base hit him. The sonofabitch ain't got a thing."

There are also appropriate curse words to use when the umpire has called you out and you're convinced you were safe; when you make an error and allow two unearned runs to score; when the manager did not pencil your name into

187

the starting lineup; and when the sonofabitch who didn't have a thing has struck you out for the fourth straight time. I'm making every attempt to keep this a fairly-clean book, however, so please use your imagination to figure out which cuss words fit which of the previously-listed situations.

I also learned a lot of clichés playing baseball — clichés that could be used later in life as well, but clichés that women never understand.

There was "can of corn," for example. When somebody lofts a lazy fly ball to the outfield, the cliché everybody uses is, "can of corn." That means it's a simple out. Later, when another man asks you, "Think you're going to score with Roxanne Smitherington tonight?", you can boast, "Can of corn," meaning, turn out the lights, the party's over.

"Caught looking" is a cliché used when a batter looks at a third strike without swinging. When a man knows his wife is running around on him and doesn't do anything to stop the illicit relationship (such as attempting to beat the other man over the head with a fungo bat) and his wife eventually ditches him for the other man, he is said to have been "caught looking."

"It'll look like a line drive in the box score in the morning," is another great baseball cliché. It also may be adapted to a sexual situation. In baseball, "It'll look like a line drive in the box score in the morning" means you have reached base safely, but you haven't hit the ball very hard. I once hit a ball off the end of my bat. It landed on the rightfield foul line spinning like a top.

The ball spun under the concession stand, and by the time the right fielder retrieved it, I was on third base with a triple. In the box score that ran in the weekly paper, however, there was a "1" by my name under the hit column. For all anybody who wasn't at the game knew, I had knocked the cover off the ball.

Now, for the sex part. Let's say a man is out with his girl and he wants to fondle her breasts. At first, she won't allow it, but then she says she'll let him feel a little, but she won't take off her blouse.

She asks, "Is that enough for you?"

And if he has played baseball at some point in his life, he answers, "Sweetheart, it'll look like a line drive in the box score in the morning." That means, wait 'til you hear how he describes what happened to his pals when he runs into them the next morning.

* * *

Playing baseball also brings men closer together. Men who play baseball together, like men who fight wars together, always have a common bond between them.

When we were ten, Danny Thompson and I went to the county seat of Newnan to try out for Little League baseball. This was official, bonafide Little League, with new balls and bats and uniforms and smooth infields with lights and grown men to coach.

We had played the game before, but only in Danny's yard or over at the school playground, where there was always only one bat and one tattered ball, with electrical tape around it, that would get lost in the high weeds three or four times an hour, forcing the game to halt for a search.

And there were never enough gloves or players to go around. We played four-on-four or, at best, five-on-five. You left the glove you were wearing in the field when it came your time to bat, and since we never had enough players to

189

have a rightfielder, if you hit the ball to rightfield, God forbid, you were out.

I wanted desperately to make the Little League team in Newnan. I was shaking in my Keds the afternoon Danny's father drove us for our first tryout.

The city kids from Newnan looked so much bigger than I felt, and some even wore regulation caps and baseball shoes with rubber cleats. We had heard that Newnan had a lot of rich people, but we didn't know they were *that* rich. Every kid had his own glove.

I got cut the first day, but Danny made the team. It broke my heart. I was ashamed that he had made the team and I hadn't, and I missed him those summer afternoons when he was in Newnan playing official Little League baseball and I was stuck at home swatting rocks with a broomstick out in the gravel driveway.

A summer later, however, I got a break. Of all the wonderful things that ever could have happened, the Baptist church in Moreland decided to sponsor a boys' baseball team, and it would play teams from other Baptist churches around the county.

Of course, I was a Methodist at the time, but I was fully willing to become a Baptist in order to make the team.

Before I could go through with my plan to switch denominations, however, the Baptist deacons voted to allow any boy in town who could run, hit, catch, and pitch to play on the team, thus saving me a dunking in the Baptist pool which always seemed to be covered with green scum, water bugs, and an occasional dragonfly.

We even were provided uniforms and new bats and new balls, and such was the excitement around town that several members of the team even received new gloves from their

190

parents. I did, too, but the story isn't that simple.

My stepfather, H.B., had been a permanent member of our household for approximately a year when the Baptist church started its baseball team. He and I were not getting on together. My real father had been a pushover, but H.B. insisted on regular chores, on regular bedtimes, and on cleaning my plate, even if we were having liver.

In contrast to my father, H.B. knew little of sport. He attempted one afternoon to play catch with me, but I quickly noticed that he threw the ball with far too much wrist. "You never played baseball?" I asked him.

"Never had time," he answered. "There isn't time for anything else but work on a tobacco farm."

I wasn't impressed. With my childlike reasoning, I even lost some respect for the man. I think he sensed that.

I had a baseball glove, but it was old and the rawhide strings that held it together were falling loose all about it. I came home from the first practice with the Moreland team in tears. I had seem all my teammates sporting new gloves. I cried in my mother's arms.

"Maybe you'll get a new glove for your birthday," she suggested.

A lot of help she was. My birthday wasn't until October.

I knew what sort of glove I wanted. I had seen it at the hardware store in Newnan. It was a fielder's glove with a deep pocket, and it was autographed by Pee Wee Reese of the Dodgers. It cost thirteen dollars. I often went to sleep dreaming of that glove.

A couple of days after my tearful scene with my mother, she told me that H.B. wanted to see me in their bedroom. I presumed the worst. He had something for me to do that would involve wheelbarrows and digging around in the dirt.

I walked into the bedroom as he was putting on his tie. "Look in the sack on the bed," he said to me.

I picked up the sack and looked inside. It was a new baseball glove, but it wasn't the glove I had wanted, the glove I had dreamed about. I had never even heard of the bush-leaguer who had lent his name to it.

"That what you wanted?" H.B. said.

"I wanted a Pee Wee Reese glove," I answered.

"Who is Pee Wee Reese?" he asked.

That settled it. The man was totally without portfolio when it came to baseball. I threw the glove down and ran to my room crying.

I'm not certain when I realized that I had done something wrong. Perhaps it was in the night sometime, when I recalled the look on my stepfather's face as he watched me peer into the sack.

He had made the move. He had known that his lack of baseball expertise had disappointed and frustrated me, so he had tried to surprise me with the new glove. He had reached out to me, but I had been ungrateful.

I never got over that awful thing I did to my stepfather — it grieves me even now — but I did attempt to make amends. I told him I was sorry. I even tried the glove. It wasn't that bad a glove. The first game we played, H.B. came. I pitched and we won. After the game, he said, "You have a nice fastball."

It is amazing what bonds baseball can develop between men ... and between boys and men.

* * *

It has been nearly thirty years, but I remember the More-

192

land Baptist lineup as vividly as ever: Danny Thompson played first; Bobby Entrekin was at second; Wayne Moore, the coach's son, was at shortstop; Danny Boswell played third; Dudley Stamps caught; Charlie Moore was in the outfield with Mike Murphy and Eddie Estes. I pitched.

Pete Moore, "Mr. Pete" to us, was the coach. He was a short, heavy-set man of great baseball wisdom and patience. Perhaps his greatest move was to devise a plan to save our supply of new baseballs.

The problem was this: We played our home games on the Moreland School playground field. There was a wire backstop behind home plate, but it wasn't much of one. Foul balls went over and through the backstop and usually landed inside a birddog pen directly behind the field.

Given the opportunity, birddogs will chew a baseball right down to the cork in a matter of seconds.

After the birddogs had chewed up enough foul balls to threaten possible cancellation of the rest of the season, Mr. Pete decided to station team reserves in the pen to retrieve the baseballs before the dogs could get to them. We called that position, naturally enough, "birddog."

That's how Eddie Estes, who later became one of the all-time great Moreland Baptist outfielders, learned to play the game. Eddie was two years younger than the rest of us. He was also a thin child but quick as a cat. And Eddie was persistent. He came to every practice and to every game, even though he never could break into a lineup made up of older boys. That was before Mr. Pete put Eddie at "birddog."

Every game, when the rest of us would head out onto the field to take our positions, Eddie would go the other way and crawl inside the birddog pen behind the backstop. The training he got fighting birddogs for foul balls eventually

193

made him into a defensive whiz.

He made the starting lineup the next season in center-field. We were playing rival Grantville, as I recall, and I was pitching. The game reached the late innings tied.

Grantville had runners on with its slugger, one of the Massengale boys, at bat. What little curve ball I had, I hung to the Massengale boy.

The ball shot toward centerfield. Eddie turned his back toward the infield and ran. There was no fence, only a gully and a dirt road that was the centerfield boundary. A few steps before he reached the gully and the road, little Eddie jumped into the air and flung his glove skyward. When he came down, he tumbled into the gully out of sight.

He quickly emerged from the muddy pit, scratched and bleeding, but the ball was in his glove. The umpire called Massengale out. We won the game.

Mr. Pete embraced little Eddie when he returned to the bench. Mays robbing Wertz in the '54 Series hadn't been as dramatic.

"Eddie," said Mr. Pete, "that was one of the best catches I have ever seen."

"I was afraid not to catch it, Mr. Pete," Eddie responded. Mr. Pete asked him why.

"I was afraid that if I didn't, you'd put me back at 'bird-dog.'"

* * *

There are instances now, of course, of girls actually play-ing Little League baseball. If she can go to her right and hit line drives, then I suppose it would be terribly unfair to keep her off the team. But I'm still old-fashioned enough

194

that I'd be shocked if I heard a nine-year-old girl, who had just struck out to start the game, come back to the dugout and tell her teammates, "The sonofabitch ain't got a thing."

What concerns me even more is, I'm not certain how many boys are playing baseball today. It seems to me that too many of them are playing soccer.

I dislike soccer immensely. It's a dull sport and it is not American. They play it mostly in those weird countries where the government changes hands every two or three days, supporting my suspicion that soccer is also a game that encourages political upheaval and anarchy.

All a person needs to play soccer is wind enough to run up and down a field for several hours and agility enough to bounce a ball off his head. Anybody can learn to run up and down a field for several hours, and I've watched seals in the circus bounce balls off their heads. On the other hand, I've never seen a soccer player who could dive underwater and come back with a dead fish in his mouth.

Kids are playing soccer all over America today, but are there any great soccer clichés? Of course not. People are too busy running up and down the field to think of any. As I explained before, in baseball there's all sorts of time to sit around in the dugout and think of clever things to say, like when an opposing player makes a stupid error and you say, "Nice move, Ex-Lax."

In baseball, you not only have to be able to run, but you also have to learn to bat and to catch and to throw and to slide and to spit. All baseball players spit. I doubt they ever spit in soccer, except when they fall down and get a mouthful of grass.

Once I was in London and, because there was nothing better to do, I switched on the BBC and watched the English

195

soccer (they call it football, which is ridiculous) champion-ship game. (After you've walked through Harrod's and been over to Buckingham Palace, London can be even more boring than soccer.)

One side would kick the ball down to the end of the field, and then the other team would kick it back. I've seen more excitement at county fair pick-up-the-duck games. The crowd, a hundred thousand or so, sang during the entire game. They apparently were just as bored as I was.

The players kicked the ball around for a couple of hours, and finally it hit a guy who wasn't looking in the back of the head and went into the goal. After much running and kicking, the guys in green finally had themselves a soccer championship by the score of 1-0.

I'm afraid that when today's young soccer players become adults, they're going to be terribly boring people and per-haps even a little fuzzy from having soccer balls bounce off their heads for so many years.

What *really* worries me, however, is the great number of today's youth who don't play baseball *or* soccer. They're in shopping malls playing those damned video games. They're all going to grow up, I fear, to have big buglike eyes from staring into too many video screens. Just listening to the infernal beeping noises those games make is enough to drive kids goofy. And trying to shoot down all those asteroids in a matter of seconds also will make a child extremely nervous and frustrated, and they may all wind up with the same bad case of the shakes overworked air control-lers get.

We played indoor games when I was a kid, too, but we played educational games like rotation pool and nine-ball, which teach a youngster such important lessons as how to

196

put reverse English on the cue ball while squinting through the smoke coming out of the cigarette he's holding in his mouth at the time.

There weren't any women allowed in pool halls, either, which offered further opportunity for male development. Girls today walk into video game arcades big as you please, and there's even a female version of "Pac-Man" — "Ms. Pac-Man," if you will.

I haven't checked to see, but if there's still a *Boy's Life* magazine, it probably carries advertisements for feminine hygiene spray these days.

* * *

One of the few remaining all-male holdouts is college fraternities. So far, women have been content to remain in their sororities. Belonging to a fraternity offers all sorts of opportunities for companionship with other men without women around. You can drink beer together and play cards together and think up nasty Homecoming floats together, and the older brothers will be available to keep you abreast of the proper way to conduct yourself as a young gentleman on campus.

I pledged Sigma Pi fraternity my freshman year at the University of Georgia. They were a great bunch of guys, the frat house was a beautiful old Southern mansion, and it was the only fraternity that offered me a bid.

Fraternity rush in my day was helpful to a young man, because it gave him the opportunity to test his fragile male ego, and it supported his theory that the more macho he acted, the better chance he had of making other young men like him.

197

Basically, rush worked like this: You walked into a large house filled with strangers. You had worn your best suit — your only suit, in my case — and you had doused yourself heavily with Old Spice, which your father wore. You went around shaking hands with members of the fraternity you happened to be visiting.

If your father had been a member of the fraternity and also was wealthy, you didn't have a lot to worry about. You probably could have managed a bid wearing pajamas and flip-flops. If you had no such legacy, then it was important that you did everything possible to make a good impression on the brothers.

"The most important thing," I had been told, "is to make certain you squeeze hard when you shake hands."

Nothing, of course, gives a man away like a soft handshake. Girls and wimps and nerds have handshakes that feel like you've just grasped a recently-departed grouper. Real men, the kind of men you would want in your fraternity, squeeze your hand firmly. Strength of grip was second only to size of genitalia in determining manhood. All this likely dates back to the days of the cave men, when they ran around naked and choked each other.

Each time I was extended a hand during rush, I made certain that I offered a firm shake in return. By the time I walked into my third fraternity house, my hand felt like a beer truck had run over it. I continued to squeeze firmly anyway, doing my best to ignore the pain and taking a certain amount of comfort in the fact that it was the handshake, not the aforementioned first measure of manhood, that was being checked.

There was something else I had been warned about when I went through rush. If you are included in a group that is

198

taken on a tour of the plumbing system of the fraternity house, that particular fraternity probably doesn't want you even to be seen on its property, much less want you to be a member.

The first house I visited was SAE. From various sources, I had learned that SAE was a very prestigious fraternity and that girls from the spiffier sororities loved to date SAE's. The SAE house was nice. I especially enjoyed seeing how the water pipes in the basement were insulated so they wouldn't freeze during the wintertime.

Next, I went to Sigma Nu. They didn't show me the pipes, but they did herd me over into a corner with two exchange students and a kid with a case of terminal acne.

I didn't do any better at Phi Delta Theta, either. One of the brothers took me and two other rushees — one of whom wore thick glasses and stuttered and the other who was wearing white socks — back to the kitchen and left us with the cooks, who were peeling potatoes.

I thought I might do much better at Kappa Sig. My first cousin happened to be chapter president. When I finally was able to corner him, however, he not only disavowed our kinship, he also swore — in a very loud voice so his brothers could hear him — that he had never seen nor heard of me before. My keen deductive senses alerted me to the fact that I might as well write off any future as a Kappa Sig.

At the Kappa Alpha house, they sang "Dixie" and told stories about Robert E. Lee. The brothers there treated me like a direct descendant of William T. Sherman. I got the pipe treatment again at Sigma Chi, and at ATO they asked me to wait out on the porch until the bus came back to pick up the rushees.

I was close to giving up on any chance at becoming a

fraternity man when I walked up the stone pathway to the Sigma Pi house, an impressive antebellum structure with large white columns and rocking chairs on the front porch. To my utter surprise, the brothers never mentioned one word about the Sigma Pi plumbing system and they seemed generally interested in me and what I had to say.

They showed me the party room and the jukebox, and they took me downstairs to something called the "Boom-Boom Room," which featured a sawdust floor, booths in which to sit, and all varieties of neon beer signs. This, I determined, was where the brothers of Sigma Pi brought their dates.

"This is probably where you bring your dates," I said knowingly to the brother giving me the tour. I might have been fresh out of high school, but I wasn't a complete dummy.

"Good thinking," said my guide. "Now, let's go over here to the toilet and see if you can figure out what we do there."

I figured I was dead after that. But, to my complete surprise, I was invited back to Sigma Pi the very next night, and when the bids went out, they offered me one. I was elated but also quite concerned. If nobody else wanted me, why would Sigma Pi, and did I really want to be a member of a fraternity that would accept the likes of me? My ego was in shambles, again.

I asked a friend, who had just accepted a bid from Phi Delt, what I should do.

"Take it," he said, "before they change their minds."

I pledged Sigma Pi and was later initiated and eventually became totally content with my membership. At my fraternity, we had a rigid code regarding responsible, manly behavior. I'll just hit a few high spots.

— AT A PARTY: Never throw up on your date. If you feel like you must throw up, go outside and do it in the parking lot. We'll make the pledges clean it up the next morning.

Never attempt to climb onto the bandstand and sing with the band until everybody is bad drunk and won't notice you making a total fool of yourself.

If you think you have the opportunity to engage in amorous activity with your date, do not take her to any of the upstairs bedrooms. We do not want coeds to see the scummy conditions in which we live.

If you have to go to the bathroom, do not go on the shrubbery outside the fraternity house. Shrubbery is too expensive to replace. Go on the tires of somebody you don't like.

— AT FRATERNITY HOUSE DINNERS: If you do not like a certain dish, such as asparagus stalks, do not hurl it at members sitting at another table. Also, do not spit English peas at tablemates and do not drink directly from the syrup container.

— WHEN PARENTS VISIT: Hide all booze, 8mm skinflicks, condoms, love dolls, firearms and explosives, poker chips, dead animals, roach collections for Saturday night roach races, and any stolen goods.

If you have any books, spread them around your room, and if somebody's parents ask your major and you can't remember, say you're undecided between pre-med and animal husbandry.

— PROPER ATTIRE: Never wear socks with your Wee-juns.

— IN CLASS: If it is absolutely necessary that you go, sit in the back of the classroom and do not ask any questions, so when you don't come back for another two weeks, perhaps

201

the professor won't notice that you're missing.

If you thought you had a copy of the exam the night before, but then the professor hands you a test that has questions you've never even heard of, pretend to have some sort of fit and maybe they'll take you to the infirmary.

— WHEN ARRESTED: Never indicate you were part of a conspiracy involving other members of the fraternity. We are a loyal brotherhood and will make the pledges fork over enough money for your bail.

My fraternity brothers were a rather diverse lot. I had one brother who rose to the presidency of the Interfraternity Council, a rare and prestigous honor. I had another who pilfered wallets. We called him "Robin Hood."

I had fraternity brothers who majored in pre-Law and pre-Med. I had others who majored in Bubber's Bait Shop and threw up on the sawdust floor in the Boom-Boom Room. I had a fraternity brother known as "Odd-Job" because of his physical likeness to the Oriental goon who was an aide to Dr. No in the James Bond movie of the same name. I was frightened of Odd-Job, especially after I saw what he did to another fraternity brother's stereo.

It was an otherwise quiet evening on the second floor of the house where Odd-Job, for the first time in his collegiate career, actually had decided to study. This was difficult for him, however, because his roommate, who was known as "Seaweed" because his father had been a famous Marine war hero, was playing Sam the Sham and the Pharoahs's "Wooley Bully" over and over again on his stereo. Several times, Odd-Job had informed Seaweed that if he didn't quit playing the record he would tear Seaweed into small pieces and let God sort them out.

Seaweed was a stubborn person, however. Also, a stupid

202

one. When Odd-Job had finally had enough of Seaweed and "Wooley Bully," he walked over to the stereo, took the record off, and began biting it into tiny pieces, spitting out the pieces directly at the startled Seaweed. Odd-Job then picked up the stereo, ripped the plug out of the wall, and threw it out the second story window, rendering it a crumpled mass of electronic innards. He had Seaweed, himself, halfway out the window when cooler heads informed Odd-Job that if he murdered Seaweed, Dean Tate probably would put us on social probation and we couldn't have a party for the entire fall quarter.

"Then, you live, swine," said Odd-Job to Seaweed. He then went back to memorizing the Emily Dickinson poem he had been assigned in English Lit class.

* * *

Belonging to a college fraternity, as playing baseball had done, provided me with wonderful memories, lifelong friends, and even the opportunity to see racial harmony at its best.

As near as I can remember, a white band never set foot in the Sigma Pi house party room between the years of 1964 and 1968. White bands simply couldn't make a party come alive and turn into a raging inferno of dancing and screaming the way a black band could.

The civil rights movement was at its peak in the early sixties, but when the music was good and the beer was cold, everybody in the party room was in it together.

It was a start to the sort of feelings that eventually led Ray Charles and George Jones to record an album together; that is the very essence of racial harmony, and music was the medium.

Fortunately, this discussion can end on a further positive note. Kids today may be playing a lot of soccer when they should be playing baseball, but I hear that fraternities and the Greek system, much maligned in the seventies, are making a comeback on college campuses. I even hear that the kids are out of Army fatigues and back into Weejuns and khakis, and that many of them are now shunning drugs for beer.

These are good signs, my fellow Americans, good signs, indeed. Not all elements of modern life have gone to hell and rust.

Now, if somebody would just tell me where I could get the sort of French fries that God intended, the kind that are cut fresh in the kitchen and have never been frozen, I might even be able to see a small, twinkling of light at the end of this tunnel. "God Save the French Fry!" Won't somebody hear my plaintive cry in the wilderness of gastronomic silliness?

13 Romancing The Turnip Green

THE FRENCH FRY is a marvelous creation. I think that perhaps God, Himself, created the French fry, say on about the twelfth or thirteenth day. And it was good. French fries stayed that way for several thousand years, but then modern man started monkeying with them.

I suspect God is quite angry about it, and that may be one reason why the weather has been so loused up lately.

Here is the way the perfect French fries should be prepared:

You take an Irish potato. You wash it and then you peel it. God didn't leave the peelings on His original French fries. That may be in the Bible someplace. Probably Leviticus.

After washing and peeling the Irish potato, you cut it into slices — not too thin and not too thick. The proper size for a slice of potato soon to become a French fry is somewhere between the size of a felt-tip pen and a baby carrot.

After slicing the potato, you drop the slices into a frying pan that has been filled with cooking oil. You fry the slices until they're sort of crispy on the outside but still nice and mushy on the inside. Some people drain the grease off their French fries once they're through cooking them, but in my estimation, the greasier the French fry, the better. And remember, God is on my side in this one.

My mother, a devout Methodist, could prepare wonderful French fries, and so could the cook at Steve Smith's truckstop, who served them with a hamburger steak that cost $1.25. Today that same piece of meat is called "chopped sirloin" and costs $6.95, and the French fries you get with it are awful. They also serve hard, dark rolls with it, rather than soft, white ones, and if you want a salad, you have to get up and go make it yourself at the salad bar. This borders on sacrilege.

I'm not sure who first loused up French fries, but I hope he's able to beg forgiveness on his death bed. One day we had great French fries — fresh and crispy on the outside and gushy in the middle — and then the next day they were all gone, and we were eating those French fries with crinkles that had been frozen.

Why would anybody want to put crinkles in sliced potatoes? Isn't it a lot of trouble? And why freeze something that's available fresh year-round?

French fries today are hard and have no flavor. All those fast-food places advertise that their French fries are wonderful, but the truth is they're terrible, a disgrace. I'll go down the list of fast-food French fries and tell you exactly what's wrong with them:

— McDONALD'S: Come on, the French fries they serve at McDonald's probably aren't even made out of potatoes. McDonald's probably has devised some scheme whereby they recycle those styrofoam containers the hamburgers

206

come in back into French fries. You know how Ronald McDonald got so ugly? Eating all those styrofoam French fries, that's how.

— WENDY'S: Wendy's French fries are not as tasteless as McDonald's, but they aren't anything to write home about, either. The only thing that makes Wendy's fries halfway edible is that compared to Wendy's chili, the French fries won't make you think you're eating something that came from the mop bucket.

— BURGER CHEF AND BURGER KING: Someday, God is going to get Burger Chef and Burger King for what they've done to His French fries. I suspect they're actually crinkle-cut zucchini.

— STEAK 'N' SHAKE: What is Steak 'n' Shake trying to do — save a few bucks by cutting their French fries into tiny, thin slices? They don't think we notice that? Steak 'n' Shake could take one potato and feed half the state of Missouri. Show me a Steak 'n' Shake French fry and I'll show you what is really a potato "stick." Remember potato sticks? They were awful, but Steak 'n' Shake is trying to bring them back. They should be ashamed.

— KRYSTAL: Krystal's home office is in Chattanooga, Tennessee, so they should know better than to serve the frozen French fries they use. I love Krystal cheeseburgers; I can eat a dozen. I hate Krystal French fries. You could put them in Wendy's chili and it wouldn't improve it.

— HARDEE'S: Worst French fries on earth. I take that back.

— ARTHUR TREACHER'S FISH 'N' CHIPS: Worst French fries on earth. So bad they had to change the name to chips. I have heard it said that even the cows wouldn't claim them.

The demise of the French fry probably began when Americans decided they didn't care what they ate as long as it was prepared in a hurry. Americans do not like to wait. They would eat French fried hog snouts if they could get them without waiting.

"Hey, Martha, want some French fried hog snouts? They taste awful, but we won't have to wait for 'em to cook."

Fast food. It has become an American tradition, like getting a divorce. First, fast food did away with good French fries. Then the hamburgers went. Somebody (probably in New Jersey) started mashing out thin, flat hamburger patties, then they froze them and shipped them all over the country to fast-food hamburger places. Because they were so thin, they took only seconds to cook, and impatient Americans flocked in and bought these mass-produced burgers.

McDonald's even went a step further and started putting a "special sauce" on their hamburgers. I don't trust anything that doesn't have a name. "Special sauce" doesn't really say what's in it. It's like the "mystery meat" Norris Brantley once ate in the school cafeteria.

Why doesn't McDonald's say it's their "special pickle relish" or their "onion-based special sauce with mayonnaise"? They either don't know what's in it themselves, or they're afraid to tell us. I've eaten a McDonald's hamburger with "special sauce" only once, and that was by mistake. It tasted to me like something you'd get if you mixed Thousand Island salad dressing and Wild Russian Vanya.

The way God intended, you don't put any sort of sauce on a hamburger, special or otherwise. What you put on hamburgers is mustard and catsup, tomatoes, lettuce, onions, mayonnaise, dill pickles, or any combination thereof.

208

And I'll tell you what else you *do not* put on hamburgers —
mushrooms. They'll put mushrooms on your hamburger if
you order one in those cutsie places where there are a lot of
house plants and they serve salads that cost up to $6.95.

I went into one of those places recently and ordered a
simple cheeseburger. The waitress asked if I wanted it on
pita bread. I didn't have any idea what pita bread was, but I
knew I didn't want it covering up my cheeseburger. I asked
for a regular bun like you're supposed to serve a cheeseburger on, and the waitress went off in a huff. She brought
the cheeseburger back on the right bun, but she also covered it with mushrooms.

"My God!" I exclaimed. "Somebody has put toadstools on
my cheeseburger."

"Those aren't toadstools," said the waitress. "They're
mushrooms. We always put mushrooms on our cheeseburgers."

"Do you know, young lady," I replied, "that these are, in
fact, toadstools, and do you know how toadstools got their
name?"

She didn't know.

"Frogs go to the bathroom under them when it's raining,"
I explained to her. "Imagine how awful it would be to have
warts on your tongue."

* * *

As long as we're on the subject of fast food, I must make
mention of biscuits, too. All the fast-food places sell biscuits
these days, and they advertise them as "just like your mother
made."

I don't like for anybody to insult my mother that way. She

certainly didn't make biscuits like those they serve in fast-food places. She made biscuits with an old-fashioned sifter and a rolling pin, and she took each individual biscuit and patted it and shaped it with her own hands. What could McDonald's know about biscuits in the first place?

As anyone with any sense knows, the only thing you're supposed to put on biscuits is either gravy or syrup. Ask some sixteen-year-old behind a McDonald's counter to put something on your biscuit, and she likely will throw on a mess of that special sauce.

Frankly, this entire McDonald's thing bothers me. Do they really know how many billions of hamburgers they've sold? Do the managers call into some central office each night to report?

"Central, this is Topeka. We sold 406 today."

"Central, Joplin here. We did 382. We dropped three on the floor, but we washed 'em off good and sold 'em anyway."

What concerns me about McDonald's and the like is that they've brainwashed our children. Kids today have grown up with fast-food food. They don't know what a real hamburger should taste like. They enjoy going to McDonald's because they see it advertised on television, because all their friends go there, because of that silly clown, and because McDonald's serves cute little food for cute little children in those cute little boxes and containers.

The Communists don't need to bomb us to take over. All they have to do is take over the McDonald's franchises one by one, and we'll fall into their hands like a ripe plum.

I have one other complaint about McDonald's — they serve fish sandwiches. What kind of person would eat a fish sandwich? What kind of fish is it? It could be monkfish or carp, for all we know.

210

I have never eaten a fish sandwich at McDonald's or at any place else. The only person I ever saw eat a fish sandwich was an ol' boy down in south Georgia one night, when they had a fish fry at a beer joint I often frequent during trips into the region.

This ol' boy walked up to where they were frying the fish, picked up a bream, put it between two pieces of white loaf bread, and ate it, bones and all.

"That's one of them Dewberry boys," the man frying the fish said. "They're hog farmers. Hog farmers will eat anything."

* * *

There is all sorts of food that confuses me today. Take one of those fifty-three-item salad bars, for example. There's the lettuce, I know that, and there are those little red tomatoes and the onions and the cucumbers in the back. (Ever notice how they always put the good stuff at a salad bar way in the back where it's hard to reach? They really don't want you to have it, that's why. They're saving it for themselves to eat after we all leave.)

But what is all that other stuff at a salad bar? Is that yellow dish an egg or scrambled squash? What about the brown stuff? Is it the house dressing or Alpo with water added? I have even seen salad bars where there were anchovies. Now, I ask you, who would put an anchovy on a salad? Have you ever looked at those little things closely? They've got hair on them; I swear they do.

The same confusion exists in other areas. I know by now that real men don't eat quiche, but what is quiche in the first place, and why isn't it pronounced "Kwi-chie" like it's spelled?

What are bean sprouts? They look like something that washed up on the beach.

One of the new items that practically every restaurant is serving today is chicken fingers. I didn't know chickens had fingers. I knew they had toes, but I didn't know they had fingers. I guess what they're really selling is chicken toes, but how much meat can there be on one of those scrawny things?

What I secretly have always wanted to be is a restaurant critic. The mistake most restaurant critics make is assuming that we're all gourmets like they are, and that we know what they're talking about when they order *Coquille St. Jacques.* I thought he was a wide receiver at LSU.

I would aim my restaurant criticism toward people like myself, who simply want to know whether or not the food is fit to eat. I would review restaurants like this:

"I walked in and this guy in a tuxedo says to me, 'Walk this way, please,' and I said to him, 'I don't think I can walk that way,' which he didn't think was very funny.

"I had myself a beer before I ordered. It was cold, but before I could tell him to stop, the waiter had poured it into a glass. Beer tastes better out of the bottle, but I suppose they don't want any bottles around in case a fight breaks out.

"I couldn't make out a blasted thing on the menu because it was all written in a foreign language. Since I was on expense account, I told the waiter just to bring me one of all the most expensive things on the menu.

"While I was waiting on my appetizer, I noticed there was butter on the table but there weren't any crackers. I like to eat butter and crackers while I'm drinking my beer. I complained and the waiter brought some crackers, but they were the kind women put out on the coffee table when they have little get-togethers, not the kind you eat with butter or with raw oysters or crumble up in your chicken-noodle soup.

"The waiter brought out the first appetizer. It smelled like the back of the supermarket where they keep the mullet on ice. It didn't taste all that bad, but I kept thinking about those mullet that still have their eyes, and they just sort of lie there in the ice on their sides with one big eye looking up at you. I was afraid there might be a fish eye in that appetizer someplace, so I just sort of picked at it.

"Then, they brought the soup. The man said it was *vichysoisse*. I complained that it was cold. The waiter said it was supposed to be. I asked, 'Well, do you have any still in the bottle?' He looked at me funny and walked off. I crumbled up some of those crackers in my soup, but it didn't help. If I wanted to eat cold soup, I'd go down to the Mission and eat what they dish out to the winos.

"Speaking of wine, I had some. It was white. 'Would you like to smell the cork, sir?' asked the man who brought the wine. I smelled it. 'That's cork, all right,' I said. Then he poured a little in my glass, and I knew what I was supposed to do then. I tasted it.

" 'Assertive, but not offensive,' I said to the wine man. That was something I heard a guy in a movie say once. I didn't have any idea what it meant, but you're supposed to say things like that whenever there's no screw-off top on the wine bottle and you aren't drinking it out of paper cups.

"I had a salad. There wasn't anything really wrong with it, except they served those little red tomatoes on it. You ever try to eat one of those suckers? If you bite down on one,

213

you'd better put the whole thing in your mouth. I tried biting one in half, and the juice shot all over a fat lady at the table next to me. I apologized and offered her what was left of my cold soup, but she declined.

"The main dish came out. It was chicken with some yellow sauce on it. After I scraped the sauce off to one side, it was passable. I didn't want to leave unless my plate was clean, so they wouldn't think I hadn't enjoyed whatever it was they picked out for me, so I took one of those hard rolls they served and tried to sop up the sauce. It's hard to sop sauce with a hard roll, I found out, so I put what was left of the sauce into my cold soup. I didn't taste it, but it looked like egg custard after I did that.

"As far as dessert was concerned, it was cheesecake and it stuck to the roof of my mouth. The whole meal cost $112.17, and I put on a big tip for everybody and said good-bye to the fat lady.

"I wouldn't go back there again if I had to spend my own money."

I could understand a restaurant review like that, but you never see them. What has happened to me in food, as in most everything else, is that I have gone back to basics.

I still eat lunch at my mother's house in Moreland once a week. She always apologizes when I walk in.

"Son, we don't have hardly anything to eat today," she says.

So what am I going to get here? A piece of toast and a radish? Then I go to the table and there's enough food to feed the Chinese infantry: country fried steak smothered in gravy, mashed potatoes with no lumps in them, all sorts of fresh vegetables from the garden, and hot cornbread and

214

maybe even some coconut pie.

People who live in towns where there isn't a McDonald's (Moreland is one of the five remaining towns on the face of the earth where there is no McDonald's. The other four are in Afghanistan) do not realize how good they have it. The dogs that eat the scraps at home eat better than I do in the city.

I don't like fancy food anymore. If the truth be known, I never did, but when I was younger I pretended that I liked it so nobody would think I was a misfit. I don't care what anybody thinks anymore.

I ate at Maxim's in Paris once. It took four guys to hand out the dessert — strawberries and cream. One guy held the bucket of strawberries, another held the dish of cream, and a third dipped the strawberries and the cream onto my plate. The fourth guy played the violin. You could buy a late-model used car, fully equipped, for what that meal cost, and yet it wouldn't touch what I can get at my mother's house for free.

This book was not designed to be a culinary guide, but because I consider myself an expert on eating (I took it up as a very young child), I'm going to offer you the benefit of my years of experience. I would ask you to clip these guidelines and attach them to your refrigerator door, but with the price of books today, maybe you should just turn down the ear of the page so whenever you're hungry or need advice about eating, you can turn to this spot readily.

GRIZZARD'S GUIDE FOR EATERS

1. Never eat barbecue in a place that also sells Dover Sole. Neither dish will be any good.

2. Never eat any place where they mark the restroom

doors in any fashion but "Men" and "Women" or "Ladies" and "Gentlemen." Especially do not eat in a restaurant that specializes in seafood and marks its restroom doors "Buoys" and "Gulls," because they have been too busy thinking up cutsie names for the restroom doors to really pay attention to the food.

3. Never eat in a restaurant where nobody speaks or understands English. You might get boiled horse or roasted dog if you're not careful.

4. As per our recent discussion, avoid any place that offers French fries and then serves you those with crinkles in them. Any place that doesn't have the decency to serve its customers hand-cut French fries doesn't really give a damn if the rest of its food is fresh and tasty, either.

5. Never eat anything that resembles a house plant, like asparagus, broccoli, or Brussels sprouts.

6. Never eat soup with chunks moving around in the bowl when you aren't stirring it.

7. Avoid "broasted" chicken. Chicken is supposed to be fried to a heavy crisp on the outside, and anybody who tries to cook it any other way is again toying with God's Master Plan.

8. Don't go into French restaurants. They charge you extra for drowning the food in all sorts of sauces. If the food was good to begin with, why would they need to put sauce on it?

9. If the waitresses are skinny, go somewhere else. If they won't eat the food, why should you?

10. Never eat in a restaurant where the maitre d' is a cop.

No. 10 deserves some further embellishment. I checked into a hotel late one Sunday evening. The hotel restaurant had been closed for hours, so I asked the lady behind the counter where I might get something to eat.

"How hungry are you?" she asked.

"I could eat the bellman's hat," I answered.

"In that case, you could walk across the street to The Cave."

"Is the food good?" I inquired.

"Let me put it this way," the woman answered. "Stephen King is thinking of basing his next novel on their menu, but you said you were hungry."

The Cave was located in the basement of an apartment building. I opened the door and the first person I saw was a policeman.

"How many?" he asked.

"One," I said.

"Are you a member?" continued the policeman.

"Of what, Officer?" I asked.

"This is a private club," I was told.

I knew all about private clubs. Private clubs are an ingenious way to get around a lot of sticky rules about selling booze after hours. The policeman explained that I could join The Cave for a dollar and have all the rights and privileges of other club members, such as being able to drink until four in the morning.

Such a deal. I paid my dollar and the policeman handed me a membership card. Then he took me to my table in a cozy little corner near the bandstand. As I was being seated, the thought occurred to me, Why is there a policeman here?

"I hope you won't take this the wrong way," I said to the policeman, "but are you expecting trouble here?"

"About twice a week," he answered, "somebody tries to cut the cook."

I considered going back to the hotel and munching on some of the plants in the lobby, but the waitress had already arrived and handed me the menu. It was printed on an air-sickness bag.

There is another rule to follow when you're eating in a place where the food is obviously of questionable quality: Order as simply as possible. As a matter of fact, that's probably a good rule to follow anytime you're eating out. I never order anything I can't pronounce.

"I'll have a steak," I said to the waitress, figuring that it's difficult for anybody to louse up a steak.

I waited for the waitress, who probably hadn't been nearly as ugly ten years and fifty pounds ago, to ask me how I wanted my steak cooked, but she didn't, so I said, "... and I would like it cooked medium well."

"Folks in hell would like some ice water, too, honey," she answered.

"I can't get my steak cooked medium well?"

"Depends on how sober the cook is," she said.

As I waited for my meal and silently prayed for at least some semblance of sobriety in the cook, I surveyed the scene around me. There were all sorts of individuals at the bar, including a very fat woman dressed in an extremely tight pair of red pants that had the words "Roll Tide," the University of Alabama war cry, written down each leg. I made a mental note to speak to the club officers about a stricter dress code for the members.

There also were several couples shuffling around the dance floor as the band blasted away. Bands that play in such places are always loud, because they follow an old musical adage: If you're going to sound terrible, do so as loudly as possible. Bands in such places always play the same songs,

218

too, and they're songs that I hate. These include "Proud Mary," "Jeremiah Was a Bullfrog," "Tie a Yellow Ribbon," and "Feelings."

The band was butchering "Proud Mary" when the waitress returned with my steak. It may have been a good steak at some point in its existence, but when it reached me it resembled a shingle. I reached for my knife. Out of the corner of my eye, I noticed the policeman move his hand toward his gun.

"I'm just going to try to cut my steak," I said. I honestly had no desire to tangle with the cook. Anybody who would do what he had done to my steak obviously was not the sort of person you'd want to face with a knife.

I had a difficult time cutting the steak. In fact, I couldn't. Finally, I asked the waitress for a couple of packages of crackers and attempted to fill up on them.

As I left, the fat girl in the tight pants winked at me.

"Roll Tide," I said, trying to be nice to a fellow member. I said the wrong thing. The band had just cranked up on "Feelings."

"How 'bout a slow dance, Sweetie?" said the fat girl as she moved toward me. I hid behind the policeman, who convinced her not to drag me to the dance floor as she obviously intended to do.

I thanked the policeman, gave him my membership card back, and made myself a promise never again to go out of town when I'm hungry. If the food don't get you, a fat girl might.

* * *

It's odd how time and circumstances change the taste

219

buds. I travel a great deal these days. Therefore, I eat a lot of airline food and hotel food (which we eventually will get around to passing laws against). But all the while, I find myself craving the food my mother reared me on. I find myself even craving turnip greens, which is a fairly complicated story with a happy ending.

I hated turnip greens when I was a child, but they were a staple for the family. My grandfather grew them in his garden and used to make me help pick them, which was like making the guest of honor at a hanging help build the gallows.

In the first place, turnip greens emit a foul aroma when they're cooking. And they do not look appetizing. As a matter of fact, they look like something that grows on top of a pond. And the very words *turnip* and *greens* are a turn-off to the appetite as well. *Turnip* sounds like something they would find growing on your pancreas.

"Am I going to make it, doctor?"

"Removing a pancreatic turnip is a serious matter, but we'll do everything we can."

Greens. That sounds like something to do with loose bowels.

"Sarah just hasn't been herself lately."

"What's her problem?"

"Got a bad case of the greens. She's been afraid to leave the house for three days."

Now that I'm older and forced to eat modern foods, however, I enjoy the occasional turnip greens that I get. My Aunt Jessie makes them for me when I visit her. Recently, Aunt Jessie had a sort of family reunion at her house, and she cooked a huge pot of turnip greens. As I was saying how tasty they were, Aunt Jessie's daughter, cousin Glenda,

220

spoke up and said turnip greens are sort of how she came to meet her new husband. I enjoy a good love story, so I asked her to explain.

"Well," she said, "I was working at a Hardee's and Owen was working at a gas station next door. One day, I stopped to fill up my tank and he came out to wait on me.

"While the gas was pumping, we started talking and I casually asked him how he was getting along. He said everything was fine, except that somebody had given him a mess of turnip greens and he didn't have a pot to cook them in.

"I said, 'Well, I've got a pot if you've got the greens,' and next thing you know, we got married."

You'll never find that moving a love story in *True Romance*. And isn't there a country music song in all this somewhere? We could call it, "You're the Greens in My Pot of Love."

* * *

Just one more note about food (which should lead me nicely into the next chapter). One of the worst things that has happened to food in the past ten years is the microwave oven. I have one in my kitchen, but it came with the house.

I worry about food that has been prepared in a microwave oven. What is a "microwave" in the first place? Does it have to do with radiation? Whenever I eat something that has been cooked in a microwave, I feel like I should be wearing a lead vest instead of a napkin at the neck.

And why do restaurants that use microwave ovens put a sign on the door that says, "Warning: Microwave Oven in Use"? Somebody told me that if you have a pacemaker in your heart and you stand around a microwave oven, the rays or waves or whatever is inside one of those ovens can throw

221

your pacemaker out of kilter. If a microwave oven can do something like that, what else can it do? My car occasionally won't start in the morning, usually after I've cooked some bacon in my microwave oven. You figure it out.

And you've heard that rumor about the woman who gave her cat a bath and then put him in her microwave to dry him, haven't you? Besides, if God really intended for us to have microwave ovens, why did He give us Ol' Diz charcoal?

Questions like that are always popping up these days. It's the price we pay for living in a world of modern technology. And just to be on the safe side, if I was a cat, I'd stay the hell out of the kitchen. Now, if everyone will kindly climb aboard the turnip truck to the next chapter, we will continue this discussion of modernity.

14 Somebody Pull The Plug On Modernity

I WAS VISITING the folks at home, and my stepfather walked outside to hang the week's wash on the clothesline. I went along for some fresh air.

The winds of early March flapped the sheets and pillowcases and the freshly-washed underwear. Both the sight and the sound were comforting, even reassuring. One of the things that's wrong with our society today, I thought as I watched my stepfather, is that most people are too pretentious to hang their underwear out to dry on a clothesline that any passerby can see.

Today, people prefer to dry their underwear inside their houses in a gadget called a dryer, which spins the clothes in vicious cycles, pumping electrically-heated air to them. As the clothes tumble, odd sounds come from the machine, and when they're finally dry, the machine stops automatically and gives out a signal that it desires to be unloaded.

But why would anybody want to be summoned by a machine?

223

Clothes dried outside by the sun and the wind and without buzzers (in Smith Barney parlance, the "old-fashioned way") have a certain feel to them. Underwear dried outside, for instance, is less likely to cause itching and, because of the natural freshness, it may not even ride up quite as readily. There's also a wonderful smell to naturally-dried clothes — the smell of the building warmth of early morning.

Maybe one reason people are more grumpy these days is that their underwear smells like coils and filters instead of like fresh sunshine. And it also rides up more aggressively, and we all know that nothing saps a person's friendliness and comfort quicker than underwear creeping into certain crevices.

Just think about a society that didn't mind hanging out its underwear for the world to see: It was a society that accepted the cards it was holding, a society that said, "My privacy is dear, but my refusal to bow to pretense is to be cherished even more." Or, put more simply, it was a society that said, "I'll hang my drawers on the line if I want to, and if mine happen to be more holey than thou's, so be it."

I wouldn't want to leave the impression that I spent an inordinate amount of my childhood staring at other folks' underwear on their clotheslines. I will admit, however, that there was occasional good sport to be had on wash day.

Miss Nellie Bascomb hung her clothes on a line in her easily accessible back yard. She wore those pink bloomers that struck just below the knee and had legs large enough for a fully-grown man to crawl through. When Miss Nellie hung out her entire compliment of bloomers, they looked like flags flapping on a mainsail.

Prissy Betty Ann Hillback, who played piano and sang solos at funerals (and who, you will remember, saved Don-

224

nelle Spinks from homosexuality), lived near Miss Nellie. One evening, a commando team of pimply-faced young men, who shall remain nameless, sneaked into Miss Nellie's back yard and took her bloomers off the line.

The raiders then slipped into Betty Ann Hillback's back yard and took her cute little step-ins, with the days of the week embroidered upon them, off the Hillbacks' clothesline and replaced them with Miss Nellie's pinks. The next morning, when Betty Ann's mother sent her out to bring in the clothes, the perpetrators of this foul deed strolled up to Betty Ann and made all sorts of hooting remarks, such as, "Hey, Betty Ann, how about loaning us a pair of your bloomers? We need a tent for a camping trip."

Betty Ann turned pinker than Miss Nellie's underpants and ran into the house. The Hillbacks, incidentally, were the first family in my hometown to buy an electric clothes dryer.

* * *

Please understand that I'm not indiscriminately opposed to modernity. Some modern inventions and conveniences, I fully condone. Here are a few:

— AIR CONDITIONING: There is absolutely no reason to sweat anymore, unless you absolutely want to, which I don't.

— AUTOMATIC TRANSMISSION: I still don't know where reverse is on a straight stick, and remember what an awful time you had with the clutch when you were stuck on a hill in traffic?

— AUTOMATIC ICE-MAKERS: Thank you, whoever invented the automatic ice-maker, for delivering me from

225

those ice trays that froze harder than Chinese arithmetic. The lever always bent when I tried to pry open the ice.

— AUTOMATIC COFFEE-MAKERS: They would be even more automatic if somebody would think of a way to make the thing remember to go out and buy the coffee, too, but you can't have everything.

— HAAGEN-DAZS ICE CREAM: I know this doesn't exactly fit here, but I love Haagen-Dazs ice cream.

— TWENTY-FOUR-HOUR AUTOMATIC BANK TELLERS: Three times a week, I run out of cash at precisely 11:30 p.m.

— BIC PENS: You lose one, so what? For a pittance, you can buy another.

— SCREW-OFF TOPS ON BEER BOTTLES: You never have to worry about keeping a church key handy again.

— OVERSIZED TENNIS RACQUETS: You don't have to bend over as much to hit the ball anymore. Bending over is something I hate about tennis.

— ELECTRIC POPCORN POPPERS: Remember when you had to shake the pot to get the kernels to pop?

— ROACH MOTELS: They don't smell up the house like Black Flag used to and they're quite effective against roaches. I checked my Roach Motel recently and found a dozen dead roaches inside, including three in the lounge and one out by the pool.

— VIDEO CASSETTE RECORDERS: This certainly is a wonderful modern invention. You can tape television programs and watch them later, and you can rent movies and watch them in your very own home. Unfortunately, I have had a video cassette recorder for four years and I still haven't figured out how to work it. I'm waiting for a fully automatic one that you don't have to monkey with and that

226

will mail off for X-rated movies on its own.

— THE THERMOS BOTTLE: A truly amazing invention. In the summertime, I put iced tea in my thermos bottle. Thirty minutes later, I pour out the iced tea and it's still cold. In the wintertime, I put hot coffee in my thermos and thirty minutes later, I pour it out and it's still hot. In the immortal words of my boyhood friend and idol, Weyman C. Wannamaker, Jr., "How do it know?"

— REMOTE CONTROL FOR TELEVISION: This invention has changed my life. Before, when I watched television, I had to sit through all those commercials because I didn't feel like getting up and switching channels. With my remote control, I can change channels any time I want without having to leave my chair.

Do you realize what this means? I haven't had to watch a Drāno commercial — the one that shows the inside of that pipe with all the hair and various other sorts of goo inside it — in years. I also haven't had to watch any commercials advertising feminine hygiene spray or mini-pads. (Has Cathy Rigby reached menopause yet? I certainly hope so.)

And hemorrhoid commercials — I don't have to watch them anymore, either. Do they still run the one where the woman is talking about her hemorrhoids and underneath her face it says, "Roxanne Burgess, Hemorrhoid Sufferer"?

I used to wonder how they found that woman. It's not the sort of thing you hold tryouts for, I don't suppose. How would you keep each contestant's score?

Do you know what *really* would be a marvelous invention? A remote control device for life. Whenever you found your-self in an unpleasant situation, you would pull out your remote control and switch around until you found a situa-tion you liked better.

227

Let's say you've been out half the night with your rowdy friends. You come home singing drunk, and your wife greets you at the door and begins calling you horrible names. Not to worry. You simply pull out your remote control and ZAP!, you're right back with your rowdy friends drinking beer and telling lies again.

* * *

So, you see, there are a few modern inventions that I enjoy, but there are many more that have weasled their way into our lives and have become great nuisances.

Take airplanes, for example. I realize that they date all the way back to the Wright Brothers, but airplanes didn't come into my life until after I was old enough to understand that anything going that fast and that high is inherently dangerous.

I fell in love with trains as a small boy. Somebody — it may have been what's-his-name, the guy who writes the daffy poems — once said, "After spending a day watching trains, baseball seems a silly game." (I just thought of his name: Rod McKuen, and that's the only thing he ever said worth remembering.)

Trains make sense to me. The engine moves and the cars attached behind it follow.

Trains are also romantic, especially their names. I mentioned earlier that I wrote a song about a train called the "Nancy Hanks." It ran between Atlanta and Savannah on the Central of Georgia line. Once, while riding the "Nancy Hanks" from Atlanta to Savannah, I drank fourteen beers in the club car — which was not that big a deal, but getting up and walking to the restroom twenty-six times on a train that is rocking back and forth may yet be a record for American railroads.

Another time I rode a train called the "San Francisco Zephyr" from Chicago to Frisco. (A "zephyr" is a west wind, incidentally.) Somewhere between Denver and Cheyenne, Wyoming, I met an Italian fellow in the club car. He spoke very little English; I spoke no Italian. I did, however, manage to get his name and to ask, "What do you do for a living in Italy?"

"I am painter," Oscar said.

See how romantic it is traveling by train? Have you ever had a drink with an Italian artist somewhere between Denver and Cheyenne, Wyoming, while traveling in an airplane? Neither have I.

"And what do you paint?" I asked my Italian friend. "Landscapes, still-lifes, pastels?"

"Houses," Oscar answered. "I am house painter."

Okay, so how many Italian house painters have you met on airplanes?

Eventually, my profession led me to travel a great deal. When you write books, you have to go many places in an attempt to sell those books. Also, people will invite you to make speeches in front of large groups (that frankly would rather have skipped the dinner and the speaker and kept the cocktail party going).

It soon became evident to me that either I would have to give up the rails as my primary mode of transportation or get a new profession, such as working in a liquor store.

In a more civilized time, a book publisher would say, "Could you be in Bakersfield, California, by Friday?" They would say that on the previous Saturday.

"Certainly," you would answer. "I can connect with the

'Super Chief' in Chicago and be there in plenty of time."

But book publishers don't say that anymore. Now they say, "Can you be in Bakersfield by five this afternoon?", and they say that at ten in the morning. And you answer, "No problem. I'll shave and shower and catch the noon flight, and with the time change, I'll be able to get a haircut at the the airport in L.A."

Anyway, the guy at the liquor store said he didn't need any help, so I had to take up flying.

The main reason I've never liked flying is that I'm terrified at the very thought of it. My friends have all attempted to make me feel better by pointing out that more people die from slipping in the bathtub than in commercial airplane crashes. If there were any way to travel by bathtub, I tell them, I certainly would do it.

If airplanes are so safe, why do they make you strap yourself in the seat? And why do they always point out, "Your seat cushions may be used for flotation"? If I had wanted to float to Bakersfield, I would have chartered a canoe.

And I still don't understand how those big suckers fly. I have a friend who is brilliant in the area of engineering and such. One day, we were riding near the airport and a large plane took off over our car.

"What makes those big suckers fly?" I asked him.

"Well, you see, there is the air foil and lift and blah, blah, blah, technical, technical...."

"I know all that," I said, "but what I really want to know is, What makes those big suckers fly?"

Faced with the option of either flying or drawing unemployment, I searched for ways to control my terror. For the benefit of others who may feel the same, here is how I cope

230

with my own fear:

— I drink a lot before getting on the plane. I'm not talking about having one drink or two. I'm talking about joining all the airlines' private clubs, where the booze is free, and drinking six or eight double screwdrivers and then calling for one of those buggies they carry handicapped people in to take me to my gate.

— I drink a lot while I'm in the air, and I ask the stewardesses to allow me to mix my own drinks, so they'll be very strong. The only problem with drinking this much is that sometimes when the airplane lands, I get off and cannot remember what city I was traveling to. So I ask and somebody tells me, but then I can't remember what I was supposed to do when I got there, so I go back to Delta's Crown Room or Eastern's Ionosphere Lounge and have another drink.

— When I have a choice, I prefer to fly with the airline that has had the latest crash. I figure my odds are better on an airline that isn't due.

— I never fly on the national airlines of Communist countries, or countries where they think cows are sacred and allow them to wander around in the streets.

— I never fly on commuter airlines. If the pilots are so good, why are they stuck flying for Air Chance ("We'll take a chance, if you will")? Besides, you know what they serve you to eat on airlines like that? The stewardess passes around an apple and a pocket knife.

— No matter what, I never go to the toilet in an airplane to do anything I can't do standing up. This eventually may lead to a very embarrassing situation for me, but I don't want them to pick through the charred remains of a crash and find me with my pants down sitting on a toilet.

— I call the pilot the night before takeoff to make certain that he isn't drinking and that he is in bed early.

— I am able to relax a bit after the seat belt sign goes off and the pilot comes on the intercom. If they've turned off the warning light and the pilot doesn't have anything to do but talk on the intercom, I figure all is well in the cockpit. On some flights, the pilot never comes on the intercom. I order another drink when that happens.

— I pray a lot. There are no atheists in a foxhole, and I doubt there are any in a 727 that is passing through heavy turbulence after takeoff from Philadelphia at night. I try never to have any dirty thoughts on an airplane, so God will like me and listen to my prayers.

Even if airplanes weren't frightening, they still would be a large pain. The food, of course, is awful; all airports are crowded; and there's usually a baby crying on every airplane (must be some sort of FAA regulation).

Planes are also frequently late, they can't take off or land in heavy fog, and sometimes too many planes are waiting to land or take off. Waiting to take off isn't that unsettling, but circling around waiting to land, knowing that a frustrated and overworked air controller is the only thing between you and a mid-air collision, is not a happy thought.

Keeping up with airline fares these days is also a big headache. I always feel guilty when I fly because I might not have gotten the best fare. You have to be careful trying to get too good a deal, however. I saw advertised recently a flight between Atlanta and New York for $26. I called the airline to inquire. The hitch was that you had to ride in a crate in the cargo hold.

Think how much better the world would be today if the

232

airplane had never been invented. There wouldn't be any threat of nuclear war. How are the Russians going to drop a bomb on us without an airplane? They sure couldn't throw it out the back of a panel truck.

And if flying had never been invented, we wouldn't have spent all that money on the Space Program, in which we sent a bunch of people to the moon to find out that it looks a lot like Nevada.

If we didn't have airplanes and still took trains, we would know a lot more about our country. You would be surprised how much of the country you can see from a train window. Did you know, for instance, that there are more piles of junk in Newark, New Jersey, than anywhere else in America?

If there were no airplanes, we wouldn't have to put up with Frank Borman, and no matter what a terrorist threatened to do, there is no way he could hijack a train to Cuba. And did you ever lose your bags on a train trip? Of course not. I took a flight between Atlanta and Charlotte once, but the airline sent my bags to Caracas.

Planes cause people to be in a rush. They cause them to go a lot of places they probably wouldn't go to if they thought about it long enough — places like Nassau and New York City and Cannes, France, where I flew to once. After about an hour, watching barebreasted women gets boring; then you have to go back to the hotel, where every Algerian and his brother-in-law is in the lobby having a loud argument.

And finally, if we hadn't been smart enough to invent airplanes, we likely wouldn't have been smart enough to invent computers, either; and I definitely could do without computers. In fact, I may be one of the last holdouts against computers, and I can prove it by explaining that I am typing these very words on a 1959 manual Royal typewriter for

233

which I paid ninety bucks and wouldn't sell for five times that, because I don't know if I would be able to find another one.

People in the swing of modern ways often say to me, "Why don't you get yourself one of those word processors? It would make writing a lot easier for you."

No, it wouldn't. First, I would have to sit for hours at a time staring at a television screen with words on it. It would be like watching one of those cable television stations where they play music in the background and words appear on the screen, giving you the news and baseball linescores.

If I watch one of those stations for longer than ten minutes, I get sick to my stomach. It's the same feeling I get when I try to read in a car.

Also, I don't know where the words go in one of those word processors. You type a lot of words onto the screen, which will hold just so many, and then they disappear. What if they accidentally went into somebody else's word processor? Not that anybody else would want my words, but some things I write never appear in print and would tend to embarrass me if somebody else were to look at them.

All of journalism has gone to computers these days. In fact, nobody types on paper anymore. When I was an editor, we had paper all over the place, especially on the floor. It gave the office a homey look. Now, there is no paper and there is carpet on the floor. I walk into a newspaper office today and I feel like opening a checking account.

When I write, I like to hear some noise. I enjoy hearing the tap-tap-tap of the keys on my Royal manual. When I hear that sound, especially if I hear it without interruption, I know I'm getting something accomplished. As with any machine, however, minor problems occasionally occur with

234

my typewriter. For instance, I once wrote an entire book without the letter "e" available to me, because the "e" character had broken on its key.

When I handed in my manuscript, the editor said, "What are all these blank spaces on your manuscript?"

"Wherever you see a blank space," I said, "that's where an 'e' goes."

There's also the small matter of maintaining a fresh ribbon in a manual typewriter, and sometimes the keys get stuck together and you get ink all over your hands trying to pry them apart. I'm constantly getting the "g," "j," and "f" keys stuck together, because I have bricks for hands. But at least my manual typewriter can't be knocked out by lightning and won't go on the fritz if I happen to spill coffee on it.

Frankly, I don't dislike computers as much as I dislike people who spend a lot of time operating them. They speak to one another in a language I don't understand, and I'm convinced they think they're a lot smarter than people who don't know anything about computers. I have a feeling that these are the same people who carried around slide rules when I was in high school and college and thought spending an afternoon discussing logarithms was keen fun.

Computers also have become an excuse. For example, "Pardon me, but is flight 108 to Cleveland on time?"

"Sorry, sir, but our computer is down."

I think what they really mean is that they have lost flight 108 to Cleveland but won't admit it. That's something else I never had to deal with when I rode trains.

"Is ol' 98 running on time?"

"She was about two minutes late into Steamboat Junction, but she's highballin' now."

Once, a large company owed me some money. It never

235

came. I called and inquired about my check.

"Our computers have been down," I was told.

"Isn't there a company officer somewhere who can simply write a check and then you could mail it to me?"

"All our checks and mailing are done by computer."

I know what they were doing. They were using my money to pay for the repairs on their stupid computers.

I'm afraid we are ruining an entire generation of Americans by getting our children involved in computers at a very young age. In some elementary schools today, kids bring their own computers to class. All I needed in elementary school was a box of crayons and milk money.

You give a kid a computer and strange things can happen. One of the little boogers eventually will figure out how to launch a Pershing missile, and try explaining to what's left of the Kremlin that little Johnny Manderson of Fort Worth, Texas, was just kidding around on his computer. I say put a twenty-one-year-old age limit on computers and send the kids outside to play ball or go drag racing. Should a kid really know his user I.D. before he knows how many fingers to hold up for his age?

My first experience with computers came when I entered college. They handed me computer cards as I enrolled in different classes. Each computer card had written on it, "Do not fold, bend, staple, or mutilate." I wondered what would happen if I should fold, bend, staple, or mutilate one of the cards.

My curiosity finally got to me, so I bent and folded and stapled and mutilated and even poured catsup on my computer card. There were no serious injuries or substantial penalties forthcoming, but it took me two quarters to get my standing as a home economics major changed.

All sorts of things puzzle me about computers:

— Computer shopping: Do we really want to shop by computer? The instant you see a TV commercial, you press a button on your computer and a conveyor belt delivers Ginsu knives to your kitchen and deducts $14.95 from your account. Could you really tell if a pair of loafers would fit by looking at them on a video monitor?

— Easy-to-use computers: That's easy for somebody else to say. I can barely operate a bottle of aspirin.

— Talking computers: Now there are even cars that talk to you. "You need gas, you need gas," says your car. Talking cars give me gas.

— Understanding computers: Where do all those cables on computers go to? Is there a little Oriental guy in a room somewhere with an abacus going a mile a minute? What's the difference between "software" and "hardware"? Is one part wool and itches a lot? Is a "semiconductor" a person who works for the railroad part-time?

— Computer dating: What if the computer doesn't mind girls who don't shave their legs and gets me a date with one? I'm the one who has to kiss her goodnight, not the computer.

— Personal computers: I don't want to get personal with a computer. I wasn't compatible with three wives. How am I supposed to be compatible with IBM?

You know something else about computers? There's nothing funny about them. In doing research for this chapter, I looked in several computer magazines. There was not a single joke section or cartoon in any of them.

The big question we must all ask is, Where is this computer business going to end? How much of our lives are they going to take over? The first computer filled a warehouse.

Now, a computer the size of your fingernail can do the same amount of computing. Will they eventually be like contact lenses, only worse? You see somebody down on their hands and knees and you say, "Lose something?"

"Yeah," comes the answer. "I dropped my computer. I know it's here in the grass somewhere."

Computers can even talk to each other now, so what's to keep them from plotting against us? And here is something else to worry about: What if all the computers on earth went down at one time? Life as we know it would come to a standstill all over the planet. The only people who would know how to carry on would be natives who live in the African bush who never have heard of computers, and me, who has steadfastly refused to learn to operate one.

Frankly, I'm sort of looking forward to that day. I could dress up in a loin cloth with my friends from the bush, and we could dance up and down and I could laugh and say, "I told you so," and poke all those uppity computer-types in their butts with my spear.

I want to get even with computers and the people who build them and the people who run them. That desire peaked recently at the airport in Jacksonville, Florida.

I was awaiting a flight. I went into the airport lounge to have my normal six or eight pre-flight double screwdrivers. There was nothing that looked unusual about the bar — just a couple of barmaids serving a weary traveler here and there.

"Can I help you?" one of the barmaids asked me.

"Double screwdriver, please," I said, "and a little heavier on the screw than the driver, if you will. The weather's bad out and I have to fly."

The barmaid didn't understand my little joke.

238

"What I'm trying to say," I explained, "is could you give me a little extra vodka and a little less orange juice in my drink. I'm nervous when I fly, and the more I drink, the more comfortable is my flight."

"All I can give you," replied the barmaid, "is what the computer shoots out."

"I beg your pardon?" I asked, somewhat in shock.

"The cash register has got this computer in it, and it's hooked up to the little hoses that we pour the liquor out of. All I do is mash the button, and the computer squirts out a shot, and it all gets rung up on the cash register."

"Let me see if I have this straight," I said. "You have no power whatsoever over how the drinks are poured? A computer measures the amount of booze I get in my drink, and there's no way you can change that?"

"Right," said the barmaid.

"In that case," I said, "bring me the coldest beer you have."

"Ain't got no cold beer," said the barmaid. "The cooler's busted."

The flight was delayed two hours because of the bad weather. I caught a cab to the nearest convenience store, bought two quart bottles of beer, and drank them out of a paper sack, eating peanuts and Slim Jims and watching the rain fall. Computerized drinking is the final straw, I thought to myself, and I prayed silently for the day that somebody, or something, would pull the plug on all this madness.

* * *

My incompatibility with modernity does not cease with

airplanes and computers. Here are some other modern conveniences that aren't.

— Telephones: Do you really think we've made a lot of progress in telephones? We haven't. Telephones, when I was a kid, were very simple to operate. You didn't even have to dial the blasted things. You just picked up the receiver, and when somebody else came on the line, you said, "Hilda, get me the courthouse."

Gossip was a lot easier to keep up with then, too, if you were on a party line. And telephone operators would make long distance calls for you, and if the line was busy, they would say, "Would you like for me to keep trying and call you back?" That was service.

I'm very confused about telephones today. I am not certain who's in charge of the telephones anymore, and there are all sorts of things you have to decide when you have a telephone installed.

Telephones used to be black. That was it. They were sort of short and squatty and black. Today, you can have a telephone in the shape of a pretzel if you so desire. A pink pretzel. "Watson, come here, you *savage.*"

Telephone numbers used to be fun, too. You dialed PLaza 7-3622, or WEird 9-6238 (if you were calling somebody in California). There weren't any area codes, either, and there were no such things as credit card numbers.

I have a friend who has one those new Sprint calling services. First, he has to dial a local number to get himself a dial tone (or should that be *punch* tone?) in order to make a long distance call. Then he has to punch in something called an "access code." Then he has to dial the number he's trying to reach.

"First," he was explaining to me, "I punch in the local

240

number, 355-0044, which is seven digits. Then I punch in my access code, which is 525-833-611, nine more digits. Then I punch in the number I'm calling, say, 1-817-423-5578. That's another eleven digits, and that's a total of twenty-seven digits. And just about the time I'm punching the last of them, my finger always slips and I have to start over."

I hate recording devices that answer telephones, too, because they entice people to create cute recorded messages.

"Hi, this is Bob. Well, actually it's not. This is Bob's machine. Bob got it from his mom for his last birthday. Mom said she was going to get Bob a puppy, but she was afraid it would just mess all over the carpet and Mom is very clean-conscious, so she got him this machine. Bob is out right now, but he will be back later, so at the sound of the tone, please leave your name and number and any message, and when Bob comes home he will call you back ... Beeeeeeeeep!"

I can't help it. Whenever I call a number and get one of those recordings, I always leave a message designed to frighten whoever owns the contraption:

"Bob, this is Davenport at the IRS, and we urgently need to see you. Do not make any plans that can't be broken for the next seven years."

Whoever invented call-waiting for telephones should be taken out and shot. Nothing infuriates me more than to be talking to somebody on the telephone when that little click goes off, and they say, "Would you mind holding for just a second?"

Damn right, I mind holding. You called me; I didn't call you.

People who have these devices on their telephones have

241

large egos. So what if somebody calls and gets a busy signal because the person is on the phone talking to me? Who could be calling that is *that* important? I suspect that they really don't work. People simply have clicking noises put in their phones so that when I'm talking to them, I'll think they're very important and popular because a lot of other people are trying to reach them.

— Showers with complicated knobs: These are found mostly in hotels. Remember how simple showers used to be to operate? There was a knob with an "H" on it and one with a "C" on it. You turned the "H" knob for hot water and the "C" knob for cold water, and you could get your shower just right.

I go into hotels now where it would take a degree from MIT to figure out which way to turn the handle to get hot and cold water. I'm surprised that scalding hasn't reached epidemic proportions in this country.

— Self-service gas stations: You go to one pump if you have a credit card, another if you have the correct cash, or another if it's Tuesday and you're wearing green slacks. I have closed deals on houses in less time than it takes to figure out how to pump ten gallons of gasoline into my automobile.

— Beepers: You can run these days, but you can't hide.

— Eyeglasses that are supposed to turn dark when you walk outside and then clear up when you go back inside: They never clear up enough when you go back inside. I had some glasses like that. Every time I walked inside a building, somebody tried to buy pencils from me.

— Talking soft drink machines: I like to put my coins in the machine and get a soft drink. If I wanted conversation, I'd talk to my car.

242

— The designated hitter in baseball: This has nothing to do with gadgetry, but it's another ridiculous modern idea. It keeps too many old, slow, fat people in the game.

— Electric shoe shiners: They don't work. When I have my shoes shined, I want to hear a rag pop.

— Beer with lower alcohol content: This allows too many sissies into good beer joints and taverns.

— Automatic pinsetters in bowling alleys: They put a lot of good pin boys out of work, and how do those things operate in the first place?

— Commodes in public places that flush automatically: I think it is my right as an American to be able to flush any commode I might be using when I'm good and ready.

* * *

There rests in most of us, I suppose, a longing for the simpler past. I'm convinced that simplicity breeds contentment, but how can one be content when constantly befuddled by a thousand different electronic gizmos that we really don't need, and by a constant stream of new ideas that don't give a national damn for tradition?

As I grow older, I become more and more comfortable ignoring these changes and trends. I don't have to do things any more just because everybody else is doing them. Who knows? Maybe by the time I'm forty, I will be able to tell somebody who wants me to be in Bakersfield by five o'clock to go stick their head in their Jacuzzi; I'm taking the train.

The thought is a delicious one.

15 You Can't Trust A Psychiatrist With Cats

I HAVE A theory about time: The longer you live, the faster it passes. When I was fifteen and wanted my driver's license more than anything in the world, it took me exactly seventeen years to reach age sixteen. After I finally became sixteen, I wanted to be twenty-one so I could go into a bar and order a beer without fearing the Gestapo would show up at my table and take me off somewhere and beat me with rubber hoses. They could have rerun the Thousand Years War during the period it took me to go from sixteen to twenty-one.

Then things began to speed up. It took about six months for me to become twenty-five; twenty-six through twenty-nine went in about a week; and the next afternoon, I turned thirty.

Turning thirty does have some benefits. For one, it means you can smoke cigars. I have never smoked cigars, but I don't think it's appropriate for anyone to smoke them until after they've turned thirty; there's nothing more obnoxious than some juvenile puffing on a big cigar and pontificating about world affairs — which inhaling cigar smoke apparently makes people do. After thirty, however, a person is finally old enough to light up a Cuesta Rey, lean back in his chair, and say the president is an idiot. Even if he is completely misinformed, people will listen to what he has to say and nod in agreement.

Another good thing about turning thirty is that you're finally old enough to realize the truth about life: It isn't fair. All young people think that Moses brought down an extra tablet from the mountain, and written on it by the hand of God was, "Life is Fair."

When my cousin got more banana pudding than I did after supper because she had eaten all her turnip greens and I had just picked at mine, I would complain to my mother, "That isn't fair."

When I was twenty-five and had cornered a beautiful young woman at a singles bar and was regaling her with my interesting tidbits of knowledge, but she wound up leaving with some guy who had large muscles and a Porsche, I turned to the bartender and said, "That isn't fair."

By the time I turned thirty, however, I had learned that what actually was written on that other tablet was, "If life had been meant to be fair, there never would have been such a thing as a proctoscopic examination."

There are some negative aspects to being thirty, of course. For example, young girls start calling you "Mister" and asking you if there was such a thing as television when you were growing up. Your parents and friends stop forgiving you for doing stupid things because you were too young and didn't know any better.

When you're thirty, you finally realize there is no chance

you're still going to be discovered by a major league scout while playing recreation league, slow-pitch softball and wind up in the big leagues and on the cover of *Sports Illustrated*.

When you're thirty, in case it hasn't happened already, you know the time is coming when you will be unable to perform sexually one evening, because your older friends have already started talking about it. The simple knowledge that it *could* happen to you will eat away at your mind, and soon that evening will come and it will go something like this:

"What's the matter?"

"I don't know."

"Is it me?"

"Of course, it's not you."

"It must be me."

"I don't know what's the matter."

"Has it happened before?"

"Of course, it hasn't happened before."

By this time, a cold sweat has covered your body and what you really want to do is hide under the bed in the dark until she leaves, and then have a nervous breakdown in private.

"Why don't we wait until morning," you say.

"I have to be up early for work."

"You don't hate me, do you?"

"Of course, I don't hate you."

"It's just that I've got a lot on my mind."

"I understand. I really do."

She doesn't really understand, of course, and she really hates you and thinks you're a wimp, and what if she goes around telling everybody? This is the stuff suicides are made of.

I had flirted a bit with adulthood before I hit my thirties. I got married for the first time when I was only nineteen. An insurance man followed me around for a month and made me feel guilty until I finally took out a policy that would make certain my bride would be kept financially secure should I die.

Should I die? The thought that I might actually die one day had never occurred to me until I took out that insurance policy. Realizing mortality is a giant step toward adulthood.

I got my first divorce when I was twenty-three. Something like that will wear off a little of your tread, too. I got married again when I was twenty-six and got divorced again when I was twenty-nine. Then something quite adult happened to me: I stopped for a few moments and had a long talk with myself to determine what it was about me that had led to two marriages and two divorces before I turned thirty.

Self-analysis is a very adult maneuver, although in my case, self-analysis did me little good. I couldn't come to any conclusions because I always was arguing with myself.

"Maybe it's because my parents divorced when I was six, and I really haven't had a role model to teach me how to fashion a happy marriage," said my ego.

"Quit making excuses. The truth is, you're a selfish, insensitive person, and nobody can live with you more than three years," said my alter ego.

"But I really tried to make a go of it."

"Tried nothing. You never tried until it was too late and you were afraid of being alone."

"I wasn't afraid of being alone."

"Yes, you were. You realized all of a sudden that if you were alone, there wouldn't be anybody around to keep your underwear clean."

"I can take care of my own underwear, thank you."

"How? You've never washed a pair of dirty underwear in your life. Your mother washed it for you and your wives washed it for you. When you weren't married and your underwear got dirty, you simply went out and bought new."

"So look what I did for the underwear industry. I'm basically a good person."

That sort of thing went on for months without resolution, so I did something that all modern adults eventually do. I went to see a psychiatrist.

I didn't tell anybody about this plan, however, because I was reared to believe than anybody who went to see a psychiatrist was admitting that he or she was some sort of screwball, soon to be admitted to a home where they would be kept very still and quiet. Milledgeville, a pleasant little village in central Georgia, was where the state sent its loonies when I was a kid. Anybody who went to Milledgeville for observation or admittance automatically was deemed completely out of focus.

The old men at the store:

"Heard about Tyrone Gault?"

"What happened to him?"

"They done took him to Milledgeville."

"When did he go crazy?"

"Said it come on him real sudden. He come in the house from the barn one day and told his wife one of his cows had just told him to go to town and buy a new tractor, and he thought it was the Almighty that was talking to him. He was back in a hour on a new John Deere."

"I heard about a fellow could make animals talk."

"You ain't never heard of no such thing. You ain't crazy like Tyrone Gault, are you?"

"Naw, it's a true story. There was this Injun and he was sittin' out by his tepee and this fellow walked up and said, 'Can your horse talk?'

"The Injun said of course his horse couldn't talk, so the fellow turned to the horse and said, 'Horse, is this Injun good to you? Does he ever put you up wet? Does he feed you plenty of oats?'

"Well, the horse spoke right up and said, 'Yeah, I can't complain one bit. He's pretty good to me.'

"The Injun couldn't believe his ears. Then, the fellow asked the Injun, 'Can your dog talk?' The Injun said of course his dog couldn't talk.

"So the fellow turns to the dog and says, 'Dog, does your master treat you all right? Does he give you plenty to eat and does he scratch your ears?'

"The dog said, 'He treats me just fine. Ain't a thing in the world wrong with the life I got.'

"The ol' Injun was amazed. The fellow asked him then, said, 'Can your sheep talk?', and the Injun said, 'Yes, sheep talk, but lie like hell.'"

"Get away from here with your foolishness."

"It's a shame 'bout Tyrone Gault, though."

"I feel sorry for his wife and children. Don't reckon he'll ever get out of Milledgeville. They say once you're down there, you don't ever get back right."

"I heard tell the same thing. I wonder what his wife would take for that new tractor?"

Even from a background of complete misunderstanding about mental health, I figured I had no choice but to seek psychiatric help. I decided, however, to pay cash for my treatments and not give my real name, in case the psychiatrist wanted to have me committed.

249

I was living in Chicago at the time, which added to the possibility that I might be crazy. I looked in the yellow pages, found a psychiatrist's office near my apartment, phoned him, and made an appointment.

I should have expected something was wrong the moment I stepped into the psychiatrist's office, which wasn't an office at all but the man's apartment. There were two cats sitting on the couch. A cat never has done anything all that terrible to me personally, but I don't like cats because they're sneaky and snooty, especially if you're a man. Women and cats seem to be able to get along together, to understand each other. Most men don't understand either one.

I sat down on the man's couch between the cats and immediately got cat hairs all over my slacks and the back of my shirt.

"Irene, you and Sparkle leave the room, please," the psychiatrist said to his cats. Not only did the man keep cats in his apartment, where they could get cat hair all over everything, but he had named them "Irene" and "Sparkle."

The psychiatrist looked a bit feline-like himself; he was thin and had beady eyes. We began by talking about my childhood. I told him about my parents' divorce and the fact that I was having problems staying married.

"Did your mother give you a lot of attention as a child?" he asked.

Yes, I answered.

"How about affection?"

I said yes to that, too. Once my mother came to school to pick me up in the third grade and she kissed me, and my friends saw her do it and made fun of me the next day at school. I didn't tell the psychiatrist that, however. He looked as if he had been a big sissy when he was a kid, so I didn't want to offend him by telling him how much I tried to avoid being connected to that description in any manner.

"Did your mother read you stories when you were a child?" he asked.

Sure, I said. "The Little Engine That Could," "Billy Goat Gruff," and "Little Black Sambo," because it wasn't considered racist and you could even name a restaurant chain after it in those days.

"Did she put her arm around you when she read you those stories?" he continued.

I honestly didn't remember.

"Don't you think that would have been a warm, pleasant memory if she had?" asked the psychiatrist.

He was getting fairly personal. I asked him his point.

"Perhaps," he began, "you have been looking for someone to share an intimate relationship with, and because your mother never put her arm around you when she read you stories, you never felt an intimate relationship with her. So now you aren't able to construct one with anyone else."

How could I overcome this obstacle, I asked the doctor?

"Perhaps we could start now," he said. "How would you like for me to read you a story?"

Whoa, Jack, I thought to myself.

The psychiatrist reached into his bookshelf and pulled out a book. "May I come sit on the couch with you and read you a story?" he inquired.

Okay, so I was a little nervous about the way my first psychiatric session was coming along, but I figured I might as well get my money's worth. The doctor sat down on the couch with me and got cat hair all over his slacks and the back of his shirt, too.

251

Then he began reading me a story. It was a story about a couple of rabbits — I remember that. It might even have been quite a good story, but I was having a difficult time concentrating. Sitting on a couch covered with cat hairs, listening to another grown man read me a story about rabbits was a unique and somewhat unsettling experience.

About halfway through the book, the psychiatrist asked, "Do you want me to put my arm around you while I read you the story?"

He had dialed the wrong number this time.

"I think that's about all the therapy I can take today," I said as politely as possible as I stood up from the couch.

"But we still have fifteen minutes left," he said.

"If it's all the same to you," I replied, "I think I'll be leaving."

"But you haven't heard the rest of the story," he insisted.

"Heard all I want to hear."

"When will we see each other again?" he asked.

I was halfway to the door by then. I threw a couple of twenties and a ten on a table and tried to figure out what was happening. The man wanted to put his arm around me and read me a story. I wondered if somebody had tried to do that sort of thing to Tyrone Gault in Milledgeville. He might have talked to cows, but I was willing to bet that Tyrone was sane enough to avoid this sort of thing.

"Probably never," I answered belatedly.

As I opened the door to leave, Irene and Sparkle appeared in the hallway. I made barking sounds and growled at them, and they ran away. If I didn't get anything else for my fifty bucks, at least I got that.

I never went back to another psychiatrist. What would the next guy want to do? Put a pair of diapers on me and make me suck on a pacifier?

* * *

I suppose I was thirty-one, nearly thirty-two, when I left my apprenticeship and became a full-fledged adult. That's how old I was the day Elvis died. After Elvis — whose music had launched my generation into another direction from our parents' — got fat and died, I realized that adulthood was squarely on me, whether I liked it or not. I was growing old and the world was driving me toward the grave. I was convinced it would be a short trip.

Although my childhood was filled with nothing more than the usual maladies — chicken pox, mumps, measles, etc. — I became a hypochondriac at a very young age. For example, since I was eleven years old and found a wart on the side of my wrist, I've been certain that I have cancer. It was a big, ugly wart, and when I heard that a change in a wart or a mole was one of the danger signals of cancer, I never took my eyes off it.

When I was fourteen, the wart suddenly went away, but then I worried about a mole on my back. I made the mistake of mentioning my fears to my mother. She suggested that when my uncle, a doctor, came to visit, we should have him burn it off.

Burn off my mole? You mean, set fire to it? This is modern medicine? I had seen witch doctors perform the same procedure on television. Cancer or no cancer, I wasn't about to go through anything like that. When my uncle came to visit, I hid in the pump house. Later, somebody told me that the way to get rid of warts and moles was to rub them with a dishrag and then bury the rag.

I followed those directions to the letter. The mole still hasn't disappeared, but you have to give these things time.

Most hypochondriacs enjoy going to the doctor. It gives credibility to their belief that they're seriously ill. But I'm a weird sort of hypochondriac. Although at various points in my life I have had (or thought I had) tuberculosis, leukemia, malaria, and several strokes, I always have avoided going to a doctor. I simply have chosen to sit in a dark room somewhere brooding over the possibility that I might be seriously ill.

Doctors and doctors' offices spook me. I hate sitting in a waiting room — not only frightened out of my wits that I'll soon find out I have only weeks to live, but also nervous about catching whatever the other people in the waiting room have.

That's another of the health problems I've had. Whenever anybody else has a disease, I automatically presume that, with my luck, I soon will have it, too.

A guy at work came down with kidney stones.

"He was fine one minute," somebody said, "and then he was in terrible pain."

I began to feel gnawing pains in my back and stomach and stayed out of work three days drinking beer (for medicinal purposes only) to flush out my kidney stone. I'm not certain if I got rid of the stone, but for three days, I felt absolutely no pain, save a severe headache that disappeared somewhere in the middle of my second beer of the day.

I knew another man who was having trouble with his prostrate gland. He said it hurt when he went to relieve himself, and that the biggest problem was he couldn't always finish, which resulted in a terribly embarrassing circumstance each time he wore khaki pants. "All men begin to

254

have problems with their prostate after they get older," said my acquaintance.

All men? Older? When I was thirty-two, I had managed to avoid doctors for years. But maybe the odds finally had caught up with me. Maybe I had it, too. I decided it was time to get a professional opinion, so I looked up another doctor in the yellow pages and made myself an appointment.

I was quite proud. I had made my own doctor's appointment without anybody forcing me to do it, and I would walk in there and face whatever medicine the doctor dished out. I thought of cancelling the appointment no more than two or three hundred times, the last of which was when the nurse stuck her head into the waiting room and said, "We're ready for you now."

I could bolt away from here, I thought to myself. It's not against the law to run out of a doctor's office and refuse to take an examination. This was something I had to pay for.

The nurse sensed my hesitancy. "Be a big boy and come on in," she said.

Women do that sort of thing to you. They question your manhood in tight situations. If I had walked out of the doctor's office, it would have been a sign of weakness, so in I went.

Did you ever notice that the doctor is never ready to examine you when the nurse says he's ready to examine you? After you get out of the waiting room, there's another wait in a tiny cubicle they call the "holding room."

It's always very quiet in there, and everything is made out of cold metal, and the chair you have to sit and wait in is very uncomfortable, and I always have the feeling that I'm being watched.

"Watch him through the two-way mirror, nurse," I imagine the doctor saying, "and see if he does anything weird."

That idea, of course, makes you even more nervous, and if you have to scratch your privates, say, you're afraid the nurse might be watching you. So you just sit there in that quiet room, in that uncomfortable chair, nervous and frightened with itchy privates.

The doctor finally came in. He checked everything, including my prostate gland.

"Bend over," said the doctor.

I bent over.

Oh, God.

"Do you feel pain or pressure?" the doctor asked me.

"Both!" I screamed.

"Is it more pain or more pressure?" the doctor asked again.

"Pain! It's pain!" I shrieked.

"Are you certain?" asked the doctor.

I was certain by now. It most certainly was pain, the worst I had ever felt.

"You can straighten up now," said the doctor.

"That's easy for you to say, doctor," I replied. "You haven't just had an intimate experience with the Jolly Green Giant's first finger."

After finally conquering my fear and going to the doctor, I decided I ought to try to do something about my problem with dentists, too. I gathered all the courage I could muster and went to have my teeth checked and cleaned.

"When was the last time you went to a dentist?" he asked me.

"I was fifteen. Why do you ask?"

"No reason," replied the dentist. "It's just that I'm going to have to use an acetylene torch to get down to where I can clean these things."

The dentist asked if I wanted gas.

"I woke up with it," I answered. "I always get gas when I'm nervous."

"I mean nitrous," the dentist explained. "It'll help relax you."

I didn't know what nitrous was, but if it would ease my terror, I would take it.

"How much do you want?" was the dentist's next question.

I said two shoulder tanks should do nicely.

When I came out of my trance, the dentist said he was through cleaning and checking my teeth and that I needed seven fillings, two caps, four extractions, and a root canal.

"Soon as my prostate clears up," I said, "I'll be back."

* * *

I remember that as a child I would read things that said, "By the year 1980....", and the "1980" would look so strange to me.

"How old will we be when it's 1980?" my friend Danny Thompson, not exactly a mathematical whiz, would ask when we were boys together.

"Thirty-four," I would answer him.

"Think we'll ever really be that old?" he would ask.

"Not before 1980," I would say.

I had a feeling even back then — and the feeling grew with each passing year — that the 1980s might be somewhat traumatic for me. The sixties were turbulent, the seventies disillusioning, and what on earth would the eighties bring?

I got married again in 1980 ... for the third time.

In 1981, I went to Europe for the first time. The trip cost

me a lot of money, and I saw a lot of cathedrals and concierges with their hands held out.

I also turned thirty-five in 1981. I awakened in a motel room in Birmingham, Alabama, on my thirty-fifth birthday. I was alone. I called practically everybody I knew and mentioned I was alone in Birmingham — that's why they hadn't been able to reach me to wish me a happy thirty-fifth birthday.

"Please don't go overboard on my gift," I cautioned them all. They didn't.

Turning thirty-five also had its ill effects on me. It depressed me a bit to know that I was only five years away from forty, but I was uplifted by the thought that I was now the age my father had been when I was born, and I could easily recall his vitality during my days on his knee. I figured I still had a ways to go before it was time to put on a baseball cap and go to the park and feed pigeons and wet my pants (an indiscretion society allows to old men with worn out prostates).

In 1982, when I was thirty-six, I made another of my infrequent trips to the doctor, and this time he did find something wrong with me. My hypochondria had been vindicated; I'd been telling people for years that I wasn't well. I soon had heart surgery to repair a damaged valve.

I was convinced I was going to die, but I didn't. So what if I don't like Boy George, hair dryers, and airplanes? I'm impressed with medical science, and if there was any sort of computer involved in helping me live through my operation and making me fit again, then I vote that's one we spare when we get around to destroying the others.

I got another divorce in 1983, and that sort of brings my confused life up to date. I'm single again. I live alone in a

258

large house with my dog. My mother is still concerned that I can't stay married and haven't produced any grand-children.

Aging in any type of world has its negative effects — the hair grays, the eyes and legs go bad, the back hurts, the hangovers linger, and the mind starts to drift. But aging in this modern world is even worse, I think, because the older people get, the more they tend to worry, and we have every-thing from the killer bees heading north from Mexico to getting wiped out by nuclear war to worry about.

Next to worry, guilt is the most obnoxious part of aging.

I have a friend named Billy. He is forty-two and feels guilty and gets depressed a lot, like I do. Sometimes, we visit each other and feel guilty and depressed together. This usually is after we've gone out the night before and done something to feel guilty and be depressed about that was a lot of fun while we were doing it.

Billy and I are both divorced; we feel guilty and get depressed about that sometimes. We feel guilty because quite often being single is a wonderful state in which to live, but it was instilled in us in a simpler time that we weren't supposed to wind up in our middle ages still acting like we were nineteen. We get depressed because we tried to do what our parents taught us to do but failed, and damned if we know what to do about it now.

We feel guilty because we really don't have all that much ambition anymore. We both have concluded that the best way to live is not to have a lot of things you worry about losing, but our parents wanted us to have it better than they did, and if we just hauled off and went and lived on a boat somewhere, we would be letting them down. We get depressed because we don't know how to deal with those feelings, either.

Depression, says Billy, often takes the form of a tall man with a hat pulled down over his eyes and wearing a raincoat. Billy calls him "Mr. D."

He starts on you in your thirties, according to Billy. "He's the voice you hear in the morning after you've been out having a great time the night before. You never hear that voice when you're younger. Your conscience is basically still clear then.

"But after you get a little older, he starts on you. You remember that Christmas song you used to sing when you were a kid — 'He's making a list and checking it twice, gonna find out who's naughty and nice'? Well, it isn't Santa Claus making the list anymore. It's Mr. D."

I've had my own bouts with "Mr. D." He gets me when I awaken in hotel rooms far away from home in the morning. He's always peering around the corner at me when I'm doing something my mother and the old men at the store wouldn't approve of. He's there when I get involved in the Sunday Morning Academy Award Theater movie and don't make church. He's there after I drink too much, and he's there when I eat animal fat, reminding me that it causes cancer.

He's there whenever there is a dilemma in my life, whenever I don't know whether to go or stay, whether to join or not to get involved, whether to use my heart or my head.

Dilemmas. Has any other generation ever had to face as many as mine has? Sometimes, in recent years, I have felt that modern life is like a giant ice cream parlor with innumerable flavors. Do I stick with vanilla or go for something more exotic? And if I eat tutti-frutti, will it make me gay?

My mother could have read me rabbit stories and hugged

260

me until I turned blue in the face, but I don't think it would have helped.

16 Maybe Someday, Rainbow Stew

FOR MOST OF my adult life, the only thing that has been perfectly clear to me has been the booze I've used to steady my nerves. You name it and it has confused me, because usually I was right in the middle of the issue, leaning towards both sides.

We could start with Vietnam. I was born a patriot of patriots, and I don't give a rat's tail for the Commies, but I also didn't want to be sent off to get shot in some rice paddy, and I didn't want anybody else to, either.

And drugs. There I was, standing off on the fringes, clinging to the cold beer in my hand while others sat in a circle and passed around a marijuana cigarette and appeared to be having a wonderful time. All I could do was seek refuge with my own kind in some beer joint, playing country music and the Bowl-A-Matic machine.

We've been all over the music. I took off after Elvis, but had I known where he and his music eventually would lead — there's a rock singer today who bites the heads off bats as

262

part of his performance — I likely would have stayed with Red Foley.

And free sex. It has its good points, but what if I get herpes?

Constant dilemma, the legacy for my generation — the In-Betweeners — is a wearisome thing, and I don't mind admitting that I'm weary of it.

God knows, I have tried my best to fit into modern life. I bought a new house a year or so ago, and it has a Jacuzzi in the bathroom. One simply has not arrived today unless one has a Jacuzzi (which sounds like the Italian word for getting bubbles up your butt).

I've been in my Jacuzzi twice. Once, I had hurt my back playing tennis, and the doctor had said that if I had a Jacuzzi, it would be a good idea to get in it and soak my back in the hot, bubbling water.

The problem came when I tried to get out of the Jacuzzi. My back hurt so much I couldn't lift myself out. I was rescued several hours later by sheetrock workers who had come to repair a hole in the wall of my bathroom — which was the result of the first time I got into my Jacuzzi and felt those bubbles in my rear. I thought there was something strange in the tub that wanted to make friends, and in my haste to get out, I fell and knocked a hole in the wall.

So if I really am that tired of the dilemmas of modern life, what can I do about it?

First, I have to come to grips with the fact that I soon will be forty, and it's time I stopped trying to understand all that is strange and new to me. By the time a person is forty, it's much too late to comprehend anything young people are doing or thinking, and we look silly when we try.

The best thing to do is what our parents did — write off

the younger generation as totally gone to hell. If you need evidence, cite the children out in Texas who put dead bats in their mouths in an effort to emulate that nut rock singer I mentioned earlier. These children had to take rabies shots for biting bats, and our parents thought we were strange because we listened to Elvis. (I hope most parents of In-Betweeners now realize that Elvis wasn't that bad after all, compared to what is happening today. If they have, then rest well, Elvis, wherever you are; all is forgiven.)

But if kids today want to eat bats, there's nothing I can do about it, so I might as well relax and worry about something I can control. Nothing that I have control over comes to mind right off, but at least that's something else I can worry about.

After I have accepted the fact that I'm out of step with modernity, I must then look for a niche in which to crawl and rest contentedly with the idea of retirement; I'm too far gone to run in the fast lane.

I don't know if I'll ever take what seems to be a drastic step for someone who has been an urban creature for more than half his life, but I do occasionally dream of going home. Back to my roots. Back to Moreland.

Somebody once said to me, "We spend the first half of our lives trying to get away from home. We spend the second half trying to get back."

Growing up in Moreland is the primary reason I am what I am — a premature curmudgeon, longing for the simple life — and I wonder if moving back would fulfill that longing.

The boys from Moreland. Some of us got away, others didn't. Dudley Stamps is still living there. He built himself a house on the land where he was reared, and he works on cars. He steadfastly refused to budge from where he was when the changes came.

He built a stereo system in his new house that piped music into all the rooms, and he issued a dictum to his wife that never, under any circumstances, would there be anything but country music on his stereo system. He caught her disobeying his order one day — she was playing a rock 'n' roll station on the radio — and that may have been one of the things that led to their divorce. At least the man had his priorities in order.

Danny Thompson and Anthony Yeager stayed around home, too, and Clyde Elrod came back. He did just what he said he was going to do; he spent twenty years in the Navy, retired, and now drives the butane truck in Moreland. I was home for a visit not long ago, and he came by to fill my parents' tank. He told me that he used to go out on a ship for days and sit there and look out on the Indian Ocean, and all he could think about was getting back to Moreland one day.

"We didn't know how good we had it growing up," he said.

I enthusiastically concurred.

The other boys from Moreland, like me, still haven't given in to the urge to return. Bobby Entrekin has a wife and a daughter and he travels, too, so I rarely see him. I've lost track of Charlie Moore. Mike Murphy has three kids and his own business, and Worm Elrod is a hairdresser.

I suppose I also should mention Little Eddie Estes. Soon after he made that marvelous catch in centerfield to save the game against Grantville, he died in an automobile accident. He was only fourteen. His mother and daddy buried him in the Moreland Methodist cemetery, about three long fly balls from the exact spot where he made the catch.

* * *

While the rest of the world went bananas, Moreland changed very little at heart. Today, Cureton and Cole's store is boarded shut, and they're trying to refurbish the old hosiery mill and turn it into some kind of museum that reflects life in the village a hundred years ago. Moreland still respects its past, and I like that.

Steve Smith's truckstop is gone, but the interstate took most of the truck traffic anyway, and that makes Moreland even quieter. There is still no traffic light and no police department, and they still have dinner-on-the-grounds at the Methodist and Baptist churches. And you still have to drive to Luthersville in the next county to buy a bottle of whiskey. It would do me good to live someplace where the nearest bottle of whiskey is a county away.

They're still neighborly in Moreland. My Aunt Una and her husband, John, live just up the dirt road from my parents. John came down sick and they didn't know what they were going to do about plowing their garden.

"One day," my Aunt Una was telling me, "we heard this commotion out in the garden, and we looked out and there was one of our neighbors — a pilot who bought a farm down here — on his tractor plowing our garden for us. I don't know what we would have done without him."

They still plant gardens in Moreland, too, and if I lived there, there would be no reason to set foot in a McDonald's again. My Aunt Jessie, who lives on the other side of my parents' house, continues to work her own garden despite her age.

I had lunch with her recently. She served fried chicken, baked chicken, baked ham, cornbread dressing, butter-

266

beans, field peas, green beans, fried okra, sliced home-grown tomatoes, creamed corn, mashed potatoes with gravy, several varieties of cake and three pecan pies she had baked herself, and a large container of iced tea. We sat under a big tree outside and feasted upon her offerings, and there was peace in the moment.

But even if I never take the final plunge and move back home, I know that Moreland is there, mostly yet unspoiled, and that settles me when I'm caught in a traffic jam or waiting for a light to change in the city, as I stand next to a kid with a ghetto blaster on his shoulder, beating out sounds to have a nervous breakdown by. In Moreland, the music you hear is that of one of the church choirs, drifting out the open windows on a soft, still Sunday morning.

And although I remain fearful that the world eventually will go crazy enough to spin off its axis and fly into space somewhere, there are, in fact, occasional glimpses of hope that manifest themselves.

We have a popular, conservative president who once played cowboy roles in the movies. Sigma Pi, my old fraternity at Georgia, was kicked off campus in the seventies, primarily because of drug use in the chapter. It currently is making a comeback. There was even a recent letter to the editor of the Atlanta papers written by a disgruntled University of Georgia student. His complaint was that the university faculty was too liberal for the mostly conservative student body.

I read somewhere that sales on white socks are up twenty percent. Pick-up truck sales have been on the rise for years, and more and more bars are selling beer in longneck bottles. There's a joint I go to in Atlanta where they have an all-country jukebox, including a complete study in George

267

Jones, and, right there on Peachtree Street in trendy Buckhead, the place is packed every night.

Tobacco chewing and snuff-dipping are in style again, and ridership on America's passenger trains is at an all-time high. There was a recent month in which there were four separate passenger train accidents, including one in New York where two trains collided head-on. One person was killed and a hundred were injured, and people who prefer planes made a big deal of it. But if I'm going to be in an accident while traveling, I still would prefer it to be on a train. Let two jets run together and see how many walk away.

Traditional clothing is in again. In fact, you're called a "preppie" if you wear button-down collars today. But I still contend there would be less crime and craziness in this country if everybody dressed nicely. You never hear of anybody robbing a liquor store dressed in a Polo shirt and a pair of khakis and Weejuns with no socks. Check police records if you don't believe me.

Some changes, like air conditioning, have been good for us all. Even people who live in the most rural areas of the country have air conditioning now. I have an acquaintance in a small town who sells air conditioning. He told me about getting a telephone call at his office from a lady who lived so far back in the country that the sun went down between her house and the road.

"She wanted to know what kind of air conditioners I had and what they cost. I was telling her about one air conditioner with this many BTU's and another air conditioner with that many BTU's. When I finished, she said, 'All I want is an air conditioner that will cool a b-u-t-t as big as a t-u-b.'"

Still, if we don't someday cut back on radical change and unchecked progress, we may all get our b-u-t-t's blown away

268

or replaced by robots. Or else we might end up taking off all our clothes and squatting naked in trees, like Crazy Melvin, from worrying about it.

Maybe it will be us, the In-Betweeners, who finally make some sense out of the world again. We're still young enough to have the energy to do it, and, as we get older, perhaps we will have the wisdom, too. We've seen the old way of life that we were reared in, and we've seen the new one that has given us ulcers; maybe we can pick the best of each and produce a world where everybody has a fair chance and an air conditioner. But salad bars will be unlawful.

And if we're able to do that — if we're able to lead the way out of the wilderness of frightening modernity and back into the land of simplicity and contentment that we knew as children — then having lived with the dilemmas will have been worth it. Somebody has to do something before the Democrats nominate Phil Donahue for president and he up and picks Billie Jean King as his running mate.

But until that day comes, play me the old songs, bring around my old friends, keep the beer cold, and constantly remind me to cling to the immortal words of the man who sings now in the void left by Elvis, Merle Haggard:

> *"One of these days,*
> *When the air clears up*
> *And the sun comes shinin' through,*
> *We'll all be drinkin' that free Bubble-Up*
> *And eatin' that Rainbow Stew."*

269

CREDITS

ARE THE GOOD TIMES REALLY OVER by Merle Haggard
(c) 1982 by Shade Tree Music, Inc.
All rights reserved   Used by permission

RAINBOW STEW by Merle Haggard
(c) 1982 and 1984 by Shade Tree Music, Inc.
All rights reserved   Used by permission

HAPPY TRAILS by Dale Evans
COPYRIGHT (c) 1951 and 1952 by PARAMOUNT-ROY
ROGERS MUSIC CO., INC.
COPYRIGHT RENEWED 1979 and 1980 and assigned to
PARAMOUNT-ROY ROGERS MUSIC CO., INC.

OLD DOGS, CHILDREN, AND WATERMELON WINE by Tom T. Hall
(c) 1972 Hallnote Music
All rights reserved   Used by permission

OKIE FROM MUSKOGEE by Merle Haggard and Roy Edward Burris
(c) 1969 Blue Book Music
All rights reserved   Used by permission

LOVE ME TENDER by Elvis Presley and Vera Matson
COPYRIGHT (c) 1956 by Elvis Presley Music, Inc.
All rights administered by Unichappell Music, Inc.
(Rightsong Music, Publisher)

WALKING THE FLOOR OVER YOU by Ernest Tubb
COPYRIGHT (c) 1941 by American Music, Inc.
COPYRIGHT renewed, assigned to Unichappell Music, Inc.
(Rightsong Music, Publisher)

I REMEMBER THE YEAR CLAYTON DELANEY DIED by Tom T. Hall
COPYRIGHT (c) 1971 by Newkeys Music, Inc.
Assigned to Unichappell Music, Inc. and Morris Music, Inc.
All rights controlled by Unichappell Music, Inc.